Posters

Bevis Hillier
Posters

STEIN AND DAY / *Publishers* / New York

Copyright © 1969 *by* Bevis Hillier
Designed by Trevor Vincent *for*
George Weidenfeld and Nicolson Limited *London*
Library of Congress Catalog Card No. 74-86914
All rights reserved
Printed in West Germany
Stein and Day / *Publishers* / 7 East 48 Street, New York N.Y. 10017
S B N 8128-1241-7

Contents

10 Pre-history of the Poster

The origins of the poster – Greek poster panels and Roman hoardings – Caxton's 1477 advertisement – hand-written posters – clandestine bills satirizing monarchy and clergy in seventeenth-century France – invention of lithography – Daumier and Gavarni's lithographic posters – Denis Auguste Raffet – Edouard Manet – development of the pictorial poster in England – the *succès de scandale* of Sir John Millais' 'Bubbles' – sensational impact of Aubrey Beardsley's 1894 poster for the Avenue Theatre – the poster becomes art form in its own right

32 The French Masters

Gulf between establishment art and popular art – academic painters as tutors and exemplars of the great posterists – the important influence of the Japanese print – Vuillard, Bonnard and de Feure – Jules Chéret, the 'Watteau of the streets', as pioneer of the colour lithograph poster – Paris in the '90s as ideal setting for poster art – the genius of Toulouse-Lautrec – his training by the academic painter Bonnat – Alexandre Steinlen – the refined workmanship and soft pastel colours of Alphonse Mucha – the Gismonda poster and the effect of Bernhardt on his work – Eugène Grasset, Métivet, Adolphe Willette – Art Nouveau – poster art beginning to influence painting

80 England to 1914

The poster as natural art form of the 'age of the stiff upper lip' – the bold, colourful designs of John Hassall and their effectiveness as advertisements – the 'Hassall dog' – Dudley Hardy's 'Yellow Girl' introduces the colour poster to England – Hardy's brilliant draughtsmanship and the variety of his inventiveness – the Beggarstaff Brothers, their advertisement and theatre bills – Phil May and Cecil Aldin – Stewart Browne – Tom Browne's blown-up cartoons – Walter Crane – Harry Furniss, *Punch* cartoonist – Albert Morrow – Will True – the subtle designs of 'Mosnar Yendis'

128 America to 1914

Origins of American poster art – powerful influence of Beardsley's designs and the posters of Scotson-Clark – New York in the '90s – Will Bradley: his brilliant covers for *The Inland Printer* and *The Chap-Book*, his sophisticated assimilation of foreign influences and elegant typography – Edward Penfield's posters for Harper's and for Stearn's Bicycles – Maxfield Parrish as 'pointillist of the pen' – his covers for *The Century* and *Scribner's* – Grasset's influence on the work of Louis Rhead – Ethel Reed's 'true poster spirit'

Introduction

'Never apologise, never explain.' Although I think this the most profound maxim for ordering human conduct since Bacon's essay 'Of Simulation and Dissimulation', I feel there are two aspects of this book which at least need explaining.

First, the reader might think it odd that more space is given to a relatively minor artist such as John Hassall than to a genius such as Toulouse-Lautrec. I have deliberately organized the book on these lines to avoid rehearsing too much the lives and works of masters fully discussed by other writers, and to give new prominence to some great posterists whose work has been neglected: William Bradley, for example, an American posterist virtually ignored by modern European critics, is one artist who emerges from this study as a really considerable figure in the history of the poster, of Art Nouveau, of black-and-white draughtsmanship and typography.

Secondly, I want to defend what some might consider an exorbitant use of direct quotation. I have never been able to understand the historian's enthusiasm for converting perfectly clear original statements into a mish-mash of paraphrase – the arrogant insistence that his subjects should speak through the muzzle (sometimes, the megaphone) of his own style. Historians of literature have always felt free to use copious quotation in illustration of a thesis; with the art historian, direct quotation can give both a good indication of the artist's motives (artists, in this respect, are more honest about themselves than politicians) and, where critics are quoted, of the contemporary view of the artist's work. The authentic voice of the men comes across: the crackling wit of Bradley, the compassionate, ruminative tone of Pryde, and the muddle-headedness and literary posturing of more than one Victorian critic. Some of the quotations are from old newspaper cuttings preserved in the files of *The Times* library and not readily accessible to the general public: in these cases, it was particularly desirable to give the *ipsissima verba*, which might then serve as a source for later writers.

In writing the book, I received most generous help from Lady (Jane) Abdy, of the Ferrers Gallery, Piccadilly Arcade, and from Mr Philip Granville, of the Lords Gallery, St John's Wood, London. I was given access to proofs of Lady Abdy's illuminating book, *The French Poster: Chéret to Cappiello*, and drew on it for some of the information in the relevant chapter of this book, which she was kind enough to read in typescript, making some necessary corrections. Mr Granville, whose stock of early posters must be the richest in any European gallery, gave continual help from the outset of my research, particularly by allowing me to have examples in his gallery photographed, and by reading the typescript.

My friends Nicholas Orme and Leslie Sherwood read the proofs, and I am most grateful for their suggestions and corrections. My father gave me an understanding of the Japanese background of the French poster, and allowed me to draw heavily on his studies of the interrelation between Japanese and European art. He read the book at every stage, and his advice led to several improvements, both historical and literary.

I owe a special debt of gratitude to Miss Joan Hassall, who allowed me to interview her and to borrow many photographs of her father.

I am grateful to the staff of Weidenfeld and Nicolson for their patience when faced with an author who treats deadlines like the seven veils. In particular I thank their editors Mr Michael Raeburn and Miss Faith Evans. I was chivvied with charm.

Miss Robyn Cooper gave most valuable help with the choosing and obtaining of pictures.

I am also indebted to Miss Victoria Brittain, Mr Paul Gunn, Mr Victor Hutchings, Mr John Murray, Mr and Mrs Richard Ormond and Mr Robin Wright.

Pre-history of the Poster

The same insistence on a decisive first act of creation as led the myth-makers of the Old Testament to represent the origin of Man as a perfectly finished example set on the earth by God, the Prime Mover, in defiance of later discovered laws of evolution, led also to more or less naïve fables about the origins of the arts. In 1775, for example, David Allan portrayed a popular neo-classical idea of the invention of painting – the Corinthian potter's daughter who drew her lover's profile by tracing his shadow on the wall. The 'first potter' was another favourite subject for speculation. One Victorian writer suggested that the first pot must have been a calabash smeared with clay; another, that a footprint, hardening in the sun on the banks of the Euphrates, would naturally suggest the idea of earthen vessels to primitive man.

It comes as no surprise, then, to encounter wild and splendid notions about the origin of the poster. One inspired Victorian felt sure it all began at Belshazzar's feast: the Great Architect of the Universe had made his will terribly manifest by the writing on the wall. *Collier's Encyclopedia* suggests that 'One of the earliest posters known in history is the Hammurabi law code. It was inscribed on a diorite stele, eight feet in length, and contained twenty-one horizontal columns above which appeared a bas-relief of King Hammurabi and the Sun God who delivered to him the laws of the kingdom. This is dated somewhere between 2067 and 2025 B C.' It also points out that the Ten Commandments were chiselled on two stone tablets.

The *Encyclopedia Americana* does not grope quite so far back; but it produces among its *incunabula* of the poster an Egyptian papyrus of 146 B C containing a detailed description of two slaves escaped from Alexandria and the promise of a reward for their finder. Charles Hiatt in *Picture Posters* (1895) cites an inscription in Greek discovered in the Temple at Jerusalem in 1872 by Clermont-Gannerau. Issued in the reign of Herod the Great, it forbids entry by foreigners to certain parts of the temple, on pain of death. Ancient Greece and Rome have also been plundered for early examples, most ludicrously by Edgar Wenlock in *The Poster*, August, 1900, who states: 'Diogenes advertised himself: so did Socrates, who was his own sandwich-man.'

Certainly with the *axones* of Greece and the 'albums' of Rome, we are approaching the modern idea of the poster. The *axones* were square columns of poster panels which were given a slow and regular rotation by an inside mechanism. On them were listed the order of contests at the public games, and the names of the competing athletes. Mute-painted hoardings (albums) discovered in Pompeii, carried inscriptions and announcements of

'The Origin of Poster Art', issued by the Chicago Engraving Company, c. 1895.

public interest such as, 'The troupe of gladiators of Aulus Suettus Gerius will fight in Pompeii the last day of May'. We even know the name of one of the posterists of Rome. Hiatt writes:

Just as Sarah Bernhardt employs the decorative skill of [Eugène] Grasset to depict her as Joan of Arc, so did the old Roman actor employ Callades, an artist mentioned very favourably by Pliny, to portray him in his favourite parts. Callades would seem to have been the Chéret of his age.

One of the most lyrical masters of this kind of vapouring was Joseph Thatcher Clarke, who wrote the preface to Edward Bella's first exhibition of posters at the Royal Aquarium, London, in 1894. 'What is Raphael's "Madonna di San Sisto" (which research proves to have been painted for the banner of an ecclesiastical procession),' he asks, 'but a superlative and transfigured sandwich-board poster?' Then there is a passage of sustained vaudeville equating medieval wall-paintings with Victorian posters:

That which the façades of medieval houses, enlivened by the figures of the patron saints of the craftsmen who dwelt therein, have been in centuries gone by, the hoardings of Paris are today. In the place of the mighty St Christopher, the maker of meat-extract now displays the image of the typical young man of the fair. In the place of St Florian, who preserves Tyrolese villages from the flames, we have the skittish maidens who moderate the blaze of the uninflammable Saxoleine or Electricine. The craftsmen's guild-signs are represented by a host of allegorico-realistic figures. Delighted children munch the chocolate sticks of the cocoa grinder, or scramble for the appetizing biscuits of the wholesale bakers. Frisky damsels powder their faces with puff-balls, or temptingly offer packets of cigarette papers, cough lozenges and purgative pellets to those who have need thereof.

All these jovial essays in the archaeology of the poster seem to have little relevance to the modern poster. The most obvious distinction is that modern posters are printed, mass-produced. Caxton's advertisement of 1477, of which a copy is in the John Rylands Library, Manchester, is the earliest surviving printed poster in English. There is proof that it was intended to be stuck on a wall or board, with the words *Supplico Stet Cedula*, translated by an eighteenth-century hand on the Manchester example, 'Pray, do not pull down the Advertisement'.

This was only twenty-seven years after the invention of printing by Gutenberg. Most posters were still handwritten. In 1539, Francis I of France issued a proclamation on the use of posters:

Nous voulons que ces présentes ordonnances soient publiées tous les moys de l'an, par tous les quarrefours de cette ville de Paris et faux bourgs d'icelle, à son de trompes et cry public. Et néantmoins qu'elles

William Caxton's advertisement of 1477, which has a good claim to be called 'the first poster'. The words 'Supplico stet cedula' have been translated by an eighteenth-century hand as 'Pray, do not pull down the advertisement'.

soient attachées à un tableau, escriptes en parchemain et en grosse lettre, en tous les seize quartiers de ladite ville de Paris es esdictz faux bourgs, et lieux des plus éminents et apparens d'iceulx, afin qu'elles soient cognues et entendues parfun chacun. Et qu'il ne soit loysible oster les dictz tableaux, sur peine de punition corporelle, dont les dictz commissaires auront la charge chacun en son quartier. (We wish these edicts to be proclaimed every month of the year, at every crossroads in this town of Paris and in the outskirts of the said town, to the sound of trumpets and shouted out publicly. They shall nevertheless be affixed to a board, written on parchment in large letters, in each of the sixteen quarters of the said town of Paris and the said outskirts, and in the most prominent and conspicuous places in the said areas, so that everyone may know and hear them. And no-one shall be permitted to remove the said boards, on pain of corporal punishment, each of the said commissioners being charged with enforcing this in his own quarter.)

By the early seventeenth century, it was not the tearing down of bills that was causing concern, but the posting of clandestine ones, often satirizing the monarchy and clergy. In 1633, the posting of bills without permission was forbidden in France.

Writing *The New Picture of Paris* shortly after the French Revolution, Louis Sebastien Mercier described how poster decoration had now begun to dominate the city, and as this valuable eye-witness account has not been noted or published by previous writers on the history of the poster, I am quoting in full the translation by Wilfrid and Emilie Jackson (1929):

13

A seventeenth-century engraving of a bill-sticker, showing the telescopic scissors-like implement used to fix the poster in a commanding position.

POSTERS ON THE WALLS

This uninterrupted series of placards, white, red, pink, green, yellow and blue, express in the first place, by their freshly affixed stamps, the power of the law; then I see them as so many magnets with power to attract all who come and go, and to keep them standing before the walls to the point of being run over by the carriages; and their gaze is fixed in this manner for the better ordering of their notions; to sharpen their intelligence and quicken their memory, and, in a word, by aid of these various documentations, to set them in the path of wisdom or experience.

Where lie the means of public instruction? In the posters. But they must be good ones, i.e. good must be got from them.

In the storms of revolution the placard is the tocsin: it assembles the factions, it makes governments tremble, inflames opinion, and every writer of placard literature has a brand to his hand.

Time was when the posted bill acquainted the public with no more than the sale, perhaps, of a country house with its appurtenances and easements; or may be with the death of some dull Cardinal, the number of bottles of old wine in his cellars and the list of his rings and apostolic jewels; or with the sailing of a ship for the ladies.

But now the posters constitute a course in human morals, politics and literature; precepts on the art of governing mankind are ranged alongside the gilded promises of lottery agents, and you may study the by-laws in between a conjuror's flourishes and the quack specifics of a pill-vendor.

They form a public library, permanent, full of instruction, with the latest publications, where no attendant is required, or reading desks, nor are there pages to be turned. It is a visible record of human acts, plans, and conceptions, however odd and fugitive. At every street corner you have a mute but eloquent notification speaking to you of your health, your fortune, your pleasures, your coming movements, and holding daily converse with you on matters of physique, diplomacy, money matters, or cooking. In the wink of an eye you are put in enjoyment of the labours of artists, engineers or pastry cooks. A short but simple analysis enables you, from the sample given, to pass judgment on the exponents of whatever science.

The jovial diner-out, the man of knowing palate, may pass by the more pedantic poster, but may gather where he shall find Bordeaux without stint, or Champagne or rare liqueurs. The busy merchant called suddenly from Paris on a business eighty leagues away, finds the lightning cabriolet quicker than his wish; or would he stay here, then behold an apartment ready for him and at hand, where he may repose like the dead. Thirty-two placards advertising public shows, always in proximity and always in competition, show us a whole populace in the assiduous service of these new temples of idleness, and prove that our pleasure resorts equal the spacious Roman circuses, and that we love sights and toys as much as those ancient masters of the world. But in Rome there were no printed posters, in Rome the deaf and dumb did not communicate with their fingers; in Rome Caesar dictated to four scribes, at once, but what of that? To-day in Paris, an advertiser

opposite Colour lithograph poster
advertising an appearance of the
New York Minstrels in the Public
Rooms, Goole. It was printed by
J. Upton of Birmingham, England.
Dating from about 1880, it is one of
the earliest effective pictorial designs;
but the lettering is separate, not
·integrated into the composition.

announces himself as dictating ten letters at a time, to ten different
persons, on as many subjects, in five different tongues, and all at the
same time.

Restaurant-keepers, and provision-merchants, cooks of doubtful
reputation, offer everywhere their table and their services. And the
young, who hunger after other delights, and have been unable to resist
the call of Spring, and whom the serpent hidden in the roses of vice has
not pricked with his poison, are warned not to despair, or be over-
grieved. Choose your Æsculapius, be born again, be wiser in future,
and avoid the glittering baits offered in the dancing saloons.

Nor may you be blind to the news – you may read it without spectacles – that cancer is giving way to the attacks of science, and that
without cautery or steel, we may extirpate at the outset this gnawing
vulture which feeds on married and unmarried. As for ruptures, elastic
bandages pursue your vision. Here is a bill-sticker on a short ladder.
What is his thick paste-brush going to unroll on this defenceless wall?
Newspaper prospectuses! Their titles are one queerer than another; all
want to reform our political notions, and teach us the true state of
affairs. The new cure for all the ills of an empire:

The more we slay, the more come to be slain.

What a fine and delightful thing, this power of passing daily judgment on men, empires and courts! To distribute blame and praise
among generals, authors and legislators! How proud we must feel in
directing posterity what to think, lest it should think wrong! How
glorious to have one's tribune over the street-post. Antiquity knew not
the placard. Antiquity is to be pitied. Our descendants will be much
better informed.

The poster covers, colours, dresses Paris one may say, at the moment
when these lines are written. And Paris may be denominated *Poster-
Paris,* and be distinguished by this costume from any other city of the
world.

These innumerable paper sheets of every shape and colour tell the
stranger that nowhere, and in no other city, are there so many people
who read, so many who write, so many people who print, invent,
speculate, indulge in commerce, so many people who promise and do
not perform.

The stamp-tax, affixed even on the appeal for a lost lap-dog, or
canary, on the poor teacher's small announcement as on the money-
lender's wide display, does not hinder the placarding of every pillar
and door-frame with posters big or little, narrow or wide: and this
ingenious tax, which might have been imposed ere now, promises rich
returns. The indirect tax, so opposed by economists, may lend new
blood to the republic.

Only two years after Mercier wrote this account of a Paris
peppered with posters, a process was invented in Munich which
revolutionized the art of the poster. Like so many other important discoveries, it was later represented as the result of a trivial
domestic accident. Aloys Senefelder (born in Prague in 1771)
jotted down a laundry list for his mother with a greasy pencil

An engraving of 1845 by Gavarni,
showing a French bill-sticker of the period.

on a piece of stone. It occurred to him that the markings on the stone could be left in relief if the rest of the surface were etched away. Further experiment led to the flat-surface printing known as lithography. That, at least, is the story Senefelder tells in his book of 1818, *Vollständiges Lehrbuch der Steindruckerei* (A Complete Course of Lithography), in which he describes how he was trying to find a cheap form of commercial printing which would enable him to publish his own plays.

The use of the lithograph, with its all-embracing range of tones, from velvety blacks to pale grey traceries, was developed in France in the early nineteenth century. Daumier was its master, and although his genius was mainly for ferocious caricature, one poster he designed for the coal depôt of Ivry (1855) was still in use in 1898, and *The Poster* issue for November of that year said it was 'not out of place on the Paris walls by the side of Chéret and Mucha's works'. But as a posterist, Daumier is less considerable than his contemporary, Gavarni. This artist was born in 1804, as Guillaume Sulpice Chevalier, the son of Sulpice Chevalier, ex-member of the revolutionary committee of the Bondy section, and of Marie Monique Thiémet, a sister of the painter-actor Thiémet, whose speciality was caricaturing monks. The young artist later assumed the pseudonym Gavarni. At ten, he was apprenticed to the old architect Dutillard, at thirteen, to the instrument maker Jecker. By 1818 he was studying integral calculus at the *pension* Butet. Later he became a student at the Conservatoire des Arts et Métiers in the *atelier* Leblanc. Mademoiselle Naudet, a print-seller on the Place du Carrousel, bought some of his sepia drawings, and published the first plate that can be traced to him, 'Macédoine'. Gavarni became an illustrator to the *Charivari*, drawing hundreds of cartoons between 1839 and 1846. In 1847 he went to London, were he was fêted by the aristocracy. A publication was started called *Gavarni in London*. In 1851 he was back in Paris, and there he remained until his death in 1866.

Gavarni was happiest when depicting the low life of Paris – *filles de plaisir* or terrible old women cooking up doubtful stews in the concièrge's box, hawking matches or sweeping the gutter – but he was himself a dandy of the Brummel or Alfred de Musset type, and several of his lithographs satirize the English milord in his long redingote with large lapels. He used a cork – a *bouchon de liège* – to give his lithographs the gracious half-tones of English steel engravings. Like Victor Hugo, he was a virtuoso of ink work: he would press a pen stroke into a maze of free and *fouetté* pencil work or in a telling blotch in the darkening of a fold. With a light scraper he would make *paillettes* and jabs of light in his shadows; and he mastered the secret of 'velvet's grey-

Tony Johannot's poster for Alfred de Musset's *Voyage où il vous plaîra*, 1843.

opposite The most sought-after of all early French posters: Edouard Manet's lithograph design for Champfleury's *Les Chats*.

ness of black'. In his life of Gavarni, Octave Uzanne writes:

> He understood chiaroscuro as Rembrandt did, and he would people the fugitive shadows at the back of a room or in a landscape with vague, fantastic beings, whose presence one rather felt than saw, just as Goya did. He delighted in long white female figures, dressed in white clothes and relieved by the blackness of their hair falling in ringlets, by their frank or mischievous eyes, by a sash, by a dainty shoe – women whose slender, tapering fingers droop languidly or hold with grace the handle of a sunshade or mingle with the fluttering ribbons. To his young men he gave strength and grace, lighting up by the gleam of face and hands the blacks in their hair and their clothing. He was the sovereign interpreter of decayed and poverty-stricken old age.

And the Goncourts have described for us his method of lithography:

> With his hand supported by a rest above the stone, which was placed upright on the easel, the lithographer at first, as though at play, indulged in a series of lines and stripes and zigzags which seemed to remove the white and shining surface of the stone. This he called 'making marble'. The ground thus prepared by this jumble of scratches, his pencil, turning and returning, produced geometrical outlines, cones and squares, and polyhedrons. Then these squares, these circles, and these cubes, becoming rubbed down, lost their indefinite masses and their inert lines, and gradually resembling human forms turned into silhouettes of men and women, emerging little by little from their vague airiness, and at each stroke of the pencil acquiring relief and light and life.

Among Gavarni's best *affiches* are those for Balzac's *La Vie Conjugale*, for the *Juif Errant*, and the *Œuvres Choisies*. All of them are very rare and valuable, especially the *Juif Errant,* of which, besides the ordinary lithograph, there is a much larger coloured version signed 'Impr. Omnicolore de Ronchon'.

Also prominent among the posterists of the early nineteenth century was Denis Auguste Raffet (born Paris, 1804, died Geneva, 1860). His career was similar to Gavarni's: at fifteen he was apprenticed to a wood-turner, at eighteen to M. Cabanel, a painter on porcelain, at six francs a day. Later he studied at an art school and in the *atelier* of Baron Gros. He gained recognition with his 348 marvellously facile illustrations to *The History of Napoleon* by de Norvins. On 6 November 1838, he produced a small poster for the book, and on 15 December, completed a larger poster for it. Tony Johannot designed posters for the *Voyage où il vous Plaira*, by Alfred de Musset and others (1843), and others for a *Don Quichotte* illustrated by himself and the *Diable Boiteux*. Edouard de Beaumont was another spirited lithographer: characteristic posters are for *Le Diable Amoureux* by J. Cazotte and for *Les Nains Célèbres*. J. J. Grandville produced

CHAMPFLEURY – LES CHATS

Un volume illustré , Prix 5 Francs
En Vente ici.

a curious placard for Balzac's *Petites Misères de la Vie Humaine*, a dramatic *Ste. Hélène*, the *Fables of Florian*, and *Scènes de la Vie Privée et Publique des Animaux*, in which an ape is shown painting with a dog for his assistant, critically watched by birds, a frog and a fish. Grandville also designed a large poster (60ins by 30ins) to advertise the *Drôleries Végétales*.

Of all the early posters, the most sought-after is naturally that by Edouard Manet, for Champfleury's *Les Chats* – a superb composition of arched black and white cats among spectral chimney-stacks. Its weakness is that the lettering, no doubt added by the printer, is undistinguished and not integrated into the design: the lesson of the Japanese print was not yet assimilated. But even in 1898, Charles Hiatt could write in *The Poster*:

Among the pioneers of the movement was Edouard Manet, who, by reason of the extent of his influence and the splendid quality of his achievement, must be accounted greater than any of these [Doré, Horace Vernet, Detaille, de Neuville]. The commanding place which is justly his in the art of our time renders his single essay in the illustrated poster of quite exceptional interest. That it was instinct with originality is proved by the accompanying reproduction. It goes without saying that every collector is ambitious of possessing a copy of it, but those who have realized their ambition are few and far between.

With Manet, the influence of the Japanese print, the Impressionist Movement, and the development of colour lithography, we arrive at the modern poster in France, of which Jules Chéret is the most prolific, and Toulouse-Lautrec the greatest, master. This is the subject of our next chapter. In the 1890s, when Chéret and Lautrec posters were being collected and widely distributed, the English posterists, in particular Dudley Hardy, succumbed to the French influence. But it is worth examining the previous development of the pictorial poster in England. In the early nineteenth century, almost all posters were still of the letterpress-only kind. This led to difficulties with some of the London bill-stickers who were illiterate and tended to stick the posters upside-down. Surprisingly, the breakaway from the non-pictorial poster was led, not by young *avant-garde* artists, but by Royal Academicians, members of that second-division Pre-Raphaelite coterie, the St John's Wood Clique. In 1871, Frederick Walker designed a powerful poster for Wilkie Collins's *Woman in White*, a stage adaptation at the Olympic Theatre. Engraved on wood by W. H. Hooper, it showed a heavily draped woman with her finger at her lips, opening a door on to a starry night – a good device for drawing the eye into the poster and for holding it there by mystery and suspense. From the first, Walker seems to have appreciated the possibilities of the hoardings: Marion Spielmann quotes him as saying 'I am impressed on doing all I can with a first attempt at what I consider might develop into a most important branch of art'. Unfortunately this was Walker's sole essay in the poster: he died prematurely in 1875, of tuberculosis. His friend Henry Stacy Marks, another member of the St John's

The first really successful pictorial poster: Frederick Walker's design for Wilkie Collins's *The Woman in White*, 1871, which was engraved on wood by W. H. Hooper. The original drawing is now in the Tate Gallery.

overleaf John Parry's Dickensian view of a hoarding near St Paul's Cathedral. It shows that in the 1840s most posters were still of the letterpress-only kind.

Poster for Pears' Soap by Henry Stacy Marks, R A, engraved on wood.

opposite Aubrey Beardsley's poster for Singer pianos, a little-publicized work which achieves its effect partly by the incongruous juxtaposition of the sophisticated *salon* pianist and the woodland setting.

Wood Clique, best known for his paintings of bedraggled storks and for his frieze round the dome of the Albert Hall, designed 'Monks Shaving' as a poster for Pears Soap. The advertisers gave it the rather inappropriate caption: '"I have found [it] matchless for the hands and complexion." *Adelina Patti.*' Although the picture is dominant, Stacy Marks's work shows no conception of what the poster should be: the message is lost. The same is true of the poster by another Clique member, G. D. Leslie (son of Constable's friend and biographer C. R. Leslie) for Sunlight Soap, or Burton Barber's design for Lifebuoy. They are simply academic sketches or *Punch* cartoons with an unobtrusive label arbitrarily attached.

Another advertisement for Pears Soap, by another Royal Academician, was the artistic (and advertising) *succès de scandale* of its time: Sir John Millais's 'Bubbles'. The original work was

SINGER

AUBREY
BEARDSLEY

NEW THEATRE, OXFORD.

In aid of the Oxford Institute & St. Thomas' Parish Schools.

THURSDAY, FRIDAY AND SATURDAY,
JUNE 7th, 8th & 9th, at 8 p.m.
Matinee on Friday, June 8th, at 2 p.m.

PYGMALION
AND GALATEA
To be preceded by
The BURGLAR & the JUDGE.

WEIRDSLY
DAUBERY

Tickets may be obtained by letter or telegram of Mr. Dorrill, at the Box Office, on and after Monday, June 4th.
For particulars see small Bills

ALDEN & CO. Ltd. Bocardo Press, Oxford.

J. Hearn's parody of Beardsley's 'Avenue' poster, signed Weirdsley Daubery, advertised an undergraduate performance at the New Theatre, Oxford, in 1894.

opposite Beardsley's poster for the Avenue Theatre, which caused a sensation when it was first posted in London in 1894. ' 'Ave a new poster', quipped *Punch*.

painted in 1886; the small boy who modelled was the present Admiral Sir William James, and crystal balls were used as models for the bubbles. Shortly after Millais had finished this soapily sentimental work, Sir William Ingram came to the studio and bought the picture for the *Illustrated London News,* as he had bought others in the past. After using the picture in the paper, the proprietors sold it (as they had every right to do) to Messrs Pears, and it was not long before Millais received a visit from Mr Barratt, Pears' manager, who brought specimens of the coloured engraving that they proposed to publish as an advertisement. Millais was not enthusiastic, but at least he had to admit that the engraving was good, and anyway there was nothing he could do to prevent the poster appearing. Millais's son, John Guille Millais, later wrote: 'The advertisement appeared; and then some of the smaller fry of the Press, "the little buzzing things that stink and sting", began to whine about the "degradation of Art", of which, in their ignorance, they found Millais guilty. These attacks he treated with contempt like a famous predecessor, who shifted his trumpet and only took snuff.' But now a more formidable antagonist took the field. In her novel *The Sorrows of Satan,* Marie Corelli made one of her characters say:

I am one of those who think the fame of Millais as an artist was marred when he degraded himself to the level of painting the little green boy blowing bubbles of Pears soap. *That was an advertisement,* and that very incident in his career, trifling as it seems, will prevent his ever standing on the dignified height of distinction with such masters in Art as Romney, Sir Peter Lely, Gainsborough and Reynolds.

Millais sent her a statement of the facts, adding, 'What, in the name of your "Satan", do you mean by saying what is not true?' From Wampach's Hotel, Folkestone, on Christmas Eve, 1895, Miss Corelli sent a gushing reply, which at least satisfied Millais and his heirs:

Dear Sir John Millais, Your letter has had the effect of a sudden bomb thrown in upon the calm of my present sea-side meditations; but I have rallied my energies at last, and I assure you in the name of Satan, and all the fallen and risen angels, that I meant no harm in the remark I put into Geoffrey Tempest's mouth concerning you. It is out of the high and faithful admiration I have for you, as a king amongst English painters, that I get inwardly wrathful whenever I think of your 'Bubbles' in the hands of Pears as a soap advertisement. Gods of Olympus! I have seen and *loved* the *original picture* – the most exquisite and dainty child ever dreamed of, with the air of a baby poet as well as of a small angel – and I look upon all Pears' posters as gross libels, both of your work and you. I can't help it; I am made so. I hate all blatant advertisement; but, of course, I could not know (not being behind the scenes) that you had not really painted it

for Pears. Now the 'thousands of poor people' you allude to are no doubt very well-meaning in their way, but they cannot be said to understand painting; and numbers of them think you did the picture solely for Pears, and that it is exactly like the exaggerated poster.

The decisive move away from letterpress-only posters had been made; but as yet, even the most advanced posters were nothing more than academy pictures with captions. Then, suddenly, 'Bubbles', Madame Patti and her shaving monks, even Walker's *Woman in White*, were made to seem archaic relics. In 1893, the newly founded *Studio* presented to the art world samples of Aubrey Beardsley's genius, including illustrations to Malory's *Morte d'Arthur*. The new prodigy must have made, artistically, the same kind of sensation as the young Disraeli when the latter rose, ringed, ringleted and with rococo gesticulation, to make his maiden speech in the commons in 1837; but, unlike Disraeli, he was taken seriously – at least by art critics who mattered. In 1894 he designed a poster for the Avenue Theatre which changed the whole idea of the poster in England. Charles Hiatt, writing in the following year, gives an idea of the impression this arrogantly simple poster made:

Nothing so compelling, so irresistible, had ever been posted on the hoardings of the metropolis before. Some gazed at it with awe, as if it were the final achievement of modern art; others jeered at it as a palpable piece of buffoonery; everybody, however, from the labourer hurrying in the dim light of morning to his work, to the prosperous stockbroker on his way to the 'House', was forced to stop and look at it. Hence, it fulfilled its primary purpose to admiration; it was a most excellent advertisement.

The most articulate mockery of Beardsley's poster was *Ars Postera*, a witty verse by Owen Seaman, published in his book *The Battle of the Bays* (1896). The best stanza runs:

> Mr Aubrey Beer de Beers,
> You put strange phantoms on our walls,
> If not so daring as *To-day's*,
> Nor quite so Hardy as St Paul's;
> Her sidelong eyes, her giddy guise, –
> *Grande Dame Sans Merci* she may be;
> But there is that about her throat
> Which I myself don't care to see.

In spite of the derision, and an amusing parody signed 'Weirdsley Daubery', designed by J. Hearn for amateur theatricals in Oxford, the point had been made: the poster was an art form in its own right. The illustrator of *Salome* must have taken a perverse pleasure in Hiatt's description of him as 'Chéret's John the Baptist'.

Two designs by Beardsley: *below* his poster for John Lane's publications, and *opposite* his design for a poster advertising *The Yellow Book*, 1894. The design was printed in dark blue on yellow paper. In a panel to the right was printed: 'Sold Here. The Yellow Book. Contents of Vol. 1, April 1894, etc'.

JOHN LANE'S PVBLICATIONS IN BELLES-LETTRES FROM THE BODLEY HEAD

The French Masters

In his first foray into art criticism (in *Le Voltaire* of 17 May 1879), Joris-Karl Huysmans, five years before the publication of his 'decadent' novel, *A Rebours*, condemned the painters of the Salon – 'their Virgins dressed in pink and blue like Christmas crackers, their grey-bearded God-the-Fathers, their Brutuses made to order, their Venuses made to measure, and their Oriental pictures painted at Les Batignolles on a dull winter's day'. He claimed that he preferred 'the crudest posters advertising a cabaret or a circus' to 'the fiddle-faddle and jiggery-pokery of the Ecole des Beaux-Arts'. If this comment was fair in 1879, how much fairer it was in the 1880s, when the radiant girls and sunset colours of Jules Chéret were seen on the hoardings, or in the 1890s, when Lautrec's masterful designs and Mucha's subtly-tinted fantasias appeared.

By aesthetic criteria (and those were the only standards he acknowledged) Huysmans was justified. There had never been, it seemed, a wider gulf between establishment art and popular art. Today, with the official acceptance of 'pop' art, we have as nearly as possible approached Zola's ideal: 'All things are the same to me,' he told Baudelaire, 'shit has the same value as diamonds.' ('But diamonds are rather rarer,' Baudelaire gently expostulated). It surprises no-one to find reverently displayed, behind the Doric façade of a famous gallery, an artist's reproduction of a soup-can, or the enlargement of a frame from a comic strip. The admittance of the contemporary commonplace to official culture was unknown in nineteenth-century France, although Champfleury (whose work *Les Chats*, as mentioned, was the subject of Manet's only poster) had made a collection of *faïences patriotiques* (peasant pottery painted with slogans and symbols in the French Revolution), and was interested in old folk songs and broad-sheets. The first time contemporary 'pop' culture was literally brought in off the streets to be preserved in the cabinets of amateurs, transferred from the riff-raff to *les raffinés*, was during the poster craze of the early 1890s, started by Ernest Maindron, whose book *Les Affiches Illustrées* is an invaluable guide to the early work of Chéret and other masters.

But the great posterists were not, for the most part, nurseried in the colour and light of Impressionism, but in the gloom of petrified academicism. At the summit of the academic establishment was J.-L. Meissonier. He was a mediocre *pasticheur* of the Dutch. Yet for him, generals would manœuvre their troops into pictogenic vistas. His death provoked international grief. Statues were set up at Poissy and in the Louvre. The German Emperor sent an official telegram of condolence to President Carnot. His paintings made huge sums: the American purchase of his 'Friedland' – a scene of triumphal horsemen bursting through minutely painted

Jules Chéret: 'Casino d'Enghien', 1890. This advertises a gala performance in aid of those whose homes had been destroyed in a volcanic eruption at Fort de France, Martinique.

33

SOCIÉTÉ FRANÇAISE
POUR LA
CONSTRUCTION
DE
CYCLES
SOCIÉTÉ ANONYME
75.000
PAPILLON
SOCIÉTÉ FRANÇAISE
POUR
LA CONSTRUCTION
DE
CYCLES
CYCLES PAPILLON
PARIS
21
Avenue
DE LA
Grande
Armée
PARIS
IMP. H. LAAS, 16, R. PIERRE-LEVÉE. PARIS

A. Bonnard, poster for Cycles Papillon.

blades of grass – moved Henry James, in 1876, to a more than usually intricate circumlocution: 'If a certain number of persons have been found to agree that such and such an enormous sum is a proper valuation of a picture, a book, or a song at a concert, it is very hard not to be rather touched with awe and to see a certain golden *reflet* in the performance. Indeed, if you do not see it, the object in question becomes perhaps still more impressive – as something too elevated and exquisite for your dull comprehension.' Degas, whose comprehension was anything but dull, was rather more pithy on the subject of this picture: 'Everything is metallic, except the bayonets.' In 1890, Meissonier made 131,000 francs at the Porto-Riche sale. A few months later, Gauguin obtained less than 9,000 francs for thirty of his canvases. It is only fair to add that Salvador Dali thinks Meissonier 'as great as Cézanne'.

If Jean-Louis Meissonier represents the nineteenth-century baroque (as Juste-Aurèle Meissonnier did the eighteenth-century rococo) W. Bouguereau led the nineteenth-century rococo. The bourgeoisie of the Third Empire, who could suffer acute moral shock at the sight of a naked ankle, enthusiastically admitted to their drawing rooms his nougat nudes and sugared cupids. Raoul Ponchon wrote:

Lorsque vous voyez Bouguereau,
Fuyez, nymphes des fontaines,
Nobles Vénus, Dianes hautaines,
Les caresses de son blaireau.

(When you see Bouguereau,
Flee in terror, nymphs of the fountains,
Noble Venuses, haughty Dianas,
From the caresses of his badger-brush.)

A modern critic has written of him: 'Tout ce que l'art académique a produit de plus détestable se rencontrait dans ces nus cireux: faire laborieux, fausse simplicité, pauvreté des formes, couleur vulgaire.' (Everything most detestable in academic art met in his waxy nudes: laborious technique, false simplicity, weak composition, vulgar colour.) Degas coined a phrase to describe these fake Fragonards and bogus Bouchers: 'C'est Bouguereauté.'

Then there was Jules Joseph Lefèbvre, who painted Lady Godiva with 'l'impudique Sarah Brown, Irlandaise volcanique' as model. He refused 75,000 francs from Coventry Museum, so that the painting could go into the Museum of Amiens as his masterwork. Or again, there was J. P. Laurens, famous for his paintings of last agonies, executions, and Merovingian funerals; E. Detaille, whose speciality was beleaguered garrisons;

J. F. Raffaëlli, who painted contemporary politicians (Degas called him 'the artist of the ante-chamber'); Paul Helleu, the slick crayonist who was a part model for Proust's Elstir; Boldini, who painted Comte Robert de Montesquiou, part model for Proust's Baron Charlus and Huysmans's des Esseintes; J. J. Henner, who only liked his nudes red-headed and would supply a flaming wig to those who weren't – he was, incidentally, a pupil of Drolling, whom legend credited with having mixed his colours with powder from the cremated heart of Louis XIV, which the profaners of the urns of Saint-Paul had sold him. Other officially honoured painters of La Belle Epoque, so well recalled in Crespelle's book *Les Maîtres de la Belle Epoque*, were A. Besnard, C. Giron, J. Béraud, Benjamin Constant, H. Gerveux, A. Cabanel, L. Gérôme, C. Gleyre, F. Tattegrain, G. Rochegrosse, A. Morot and L. Bonnat.

The styles of these painters were the equivalent of what, in literature, we call 'fustian'. Yet they were the tutors and exemplars of the great posterists. In his biography of his father, Mr Jiří Mucha says: 'If we look at the past through the art galleries, we have a distorted impression of the 'eighties. It was not an ideal world of Renoir girls and Degas ballerinas, but rather one of pompous bourgeois who admired Cabanel, Gérôme and Bouguereau.' According to Maurice Denis, 'even the boldest of the students knew next to nothing about Impressionism. They admired Bastien Lepage, spoke with respect of Puvis de Chavannes (although secretly doubting whether he could draw) discussed Péladan and Wagner, read superficial, decadent literature and got excited about mysticism, the Cabbala and the Chaldean calendar.' Mucha himself, like so many other posterists, French and English, studied at the Académie Julian, in his case under Lefèbvre, Boulanger and Laurens. He was a friend and at one time a fellow lodger of Gauguin, but Gauguin had nothing to teach him in art; Mucha preferred the mystical Czech baroque tradition of his childhood, and the rigorous academic training of his youth, to Gauguin's primitivism. 'They were wild savages,' he later told his son, disapprovingly, of the Gauguin set. Chéret, Bonnard, Hassall, Hardy and Pryde were among the posterists who trained under Bouguereau. And posterists, too, could receive official honours: in 1889 Chéret was awarded the Légion d'Honneur for 'creating a new branch of art, by applying art to commercial and industrial printing'.

If we look at the subject matter of Chéret's posters, girls in tumbling petticoats brandishing Dubonnet bottles, smiling archly under light from Saxoléine lamp oil, or flirtatiously pouring 'Pippermint' by Get Frères into a thimble glass, we find that there is little difference, in the basic conception, between them and the nineteenth-century rococo of Bouguereau, or the riant

opposite Jules Chéret, poster for Saxoléine lamp oil, 1896.

Saxoléine
PÉTROLE DE SÛRETÉ
EXTRA-BLANC · DÉODORISÉ · ININFLAMMABLE
en Bidons Plombés de 5 litres
IMP. CHAIX

Henri de Toulouse-Lautrec, poster
for Bella confetti, 1894.

rococo of Carpeaux's Opéra sculptures (which were in their
turn, however, to inspire a revolutionary adaptation by Rodin
and Dalou). What distinguishes Chéret's designs from Bouguereau's blancmangy works is their colour – shameless scarlets,
blues and yellows – and the principle of flats of colour within
a strong outline: the very qualities Bouguereau's badger-brush
was designed to muzz out of existence. Chéret's rococo girls came
from the tradition of French painting – especially Watteau, whose
paintings he studied for hours in the Louvre – and Boucher,
Fragonard, and even Bouguereau, his master. But his colour
came from England, which he visited in the 1850s. Constable is
rightly regarded as the great English influence on French art; but
it was the paintings of Turner that captivated Chéret. The colours
of a Chéret poster are extraordinarily close to those of a Turner
Venetian sunset; there is the same impression of floods of natural
colour spilt with perfect control. In England also, Chéret learnt
the means of mass-producing his colour designs. He came across
a modernized version of the machinery invented by Senefelder
for processing colour lithography, introduced it in Paris, and in
1872 designed his poster for the Bal Valentino. Colour printing
had already been highly developed, in the wallpapers of Zuber
and Dufour et Leroy: but the complicated processes – some papers
were printed in eighty different colours – were prohibitively expensive. Chéret's method, using only four or five coloured blocks,
was cheap: Maindron estimated that the cost of printing a
thousand large posters was about one franc each.

The other revolutionary aspect of Chéret's posters – the
simplicity of a flat, outlined design without 'moulding' or
chiaroscuro – he took from the Japanese. The Japanese woodblock
print was the greatest determining influence on the French poster
of the 1880s and 1890s. Like the lithograph poster, the Japanese
colour print was printed from a small number of blocks. The outline, the basis or key-block of the print, was cut in relief on
cherry wood, and though the Japanese cutters were incredibly
skilful and could, even on relatively soft wood like cherry (as opposed to a hard wood such as boxwood), cut lines of a hair-
breadth's thickness, their publishers usually saw to it that the line
was strong and coarse, to obtain the maximum of impressions before the block was worn down. The blocks for colour, too, were
printed on cherry wood, which permitted large areas of single colours, the pigments being painted on to the blocks and printed flat
by burnishing the back of the paper when it was laid over the
blocks. The thickness of the outline and the flatness of the colour
areas imposed a simplicity on the design and inhibited anything
approaching the realism that had been the aim of Western artists.
But also, there was an anti-chiaroscuro tradition in the East.

opposite Jules Chéret: 'Pantomimes Lumineuses', 1892, a proof of the poster for E. Reynaud's théâtre optique, before the main lettering has been added.

The courtesan Hitomoto of Daimonji-ya, a Japanese print by Utamaro. Japanese prints influenced the poster styles of many French artists, especially Lautrec.

Western artists, especially since Rembrandt, had seen their subjects in terms of light and shade. But the Oriental eye did not see things that way: Mr James Laver has told of the Chinese connoisseur who, presented with a European portrait, asked, quite innocently, why one half of the lady's face was black. The non-chiaroscuro design was more practical technically; it was also more effective for advertising purposes, as great sweeps of colour could be shown, unmasked by 'academy brown sauce', or by grey and black shadow. The Japanese print artists were, for the most part, not free agents. They were expected to give a picture that reflected some place or person prominent in the capital, Edo: the popular teahouse, the courtesan, the star of the latest hit at the Kabuki theatre, the champion sumo wrestler. So the print was close to the Western poster in purpose.

The other thing the Japanese print taught French artists was that great artists did not have to use all their talents in depicting noble scenes of the past, in celebrating contemporary battle triumphs or painting straight portraits without an element of caricature. Artists such as Hokusai, Utamaro and Hiroshige, belonged to the Ukiyo-e, or 'Floating World' school: their object was to depict the passing show, which could include the commercial, the risqué, or the thoroughgoing erotic. That the poster got away from the sentimental and heavily comic to the racy and picaresque and the idea of 'selling through sex', must be partly attributed to the influence of the Japanese print.

Japanese prints were used as packing for the porcelain which was sent to the European market in the middle of the nineteenth century. The first Frenchman to appreciate their importance was the etcher Félix Bracquemond, who later decorated pottery in a style very reminiscent of Hokusai. In 1862, Madame de Soye and her husband opened an Oriental shop in the arcades of the Rue de Rivoli in Paris. The Pennells in their *Life of Whistler* record that Manet, Fantin Latour, Tissot, Baudelaire, Solon and the Goncourt brothers were among the early customers. Whistler was also one; he took back some blue pots and Japanese prints to London and inspired Rossetti with his enthusiasm. The early influence on European art was superficial. One can discount altogether the borrowings of subject matter from Japan – what Swinburne called 'the fairyland of fans, the paradise of pipkins, the limbo of blue china, screens, pots, plates, jars, joss-houses, and all the fortuitous frippery of Fusiyama.' Such paintings as Monet's 'Portrait with Fans' and Whistler's 'Princesse au Pays de la Porcelaine' owe an all too obvious debt to Japan, but not to Japanese art. Monet was too dedicated to capturing the effects of light to profit from a lesson in studied pattern. Whistler, even in his 'Old Battersea Bridge', which is reminiscent of Hiroshige's

Two designs by Jules Chéret.
They show his skill in capturing movement and
animation with a few deft strokes and brusque shading.

Henri de Toulouse-Lautrec: two proofs and the final version of a poster for *Reine de Joie* by Victor Joze, 1892.

'Great Bridge in Edo', still relied on a general formlessness to suggest atmosphere – quite foreign to Hiroshige's prints where the colour was imprisoned by an uncompromising black line. Whistler caught the *chic* of Japanese art, down to his butterfly seal based on the *kakihan*, but he missed its essence, except in the theory of his 'Ten O'Clock Lecture'.

Among the first European artists who understood the art of the Japanese print, and benefited from it, were Van Gogh, Gauguin and above all Toulouse-Lautrec. Gauguin and Van Gogh were immensely attracted by the landscapes of Hokusai and Hiroshige, and showed themselves prepared to sacrifice naturalism, as it had been understood for so long in Europe. Both used violent non-representational colour and what academic critics called an 'unnatural' outline. In fact, both went considerably further than any Japanese artist would have allowed. We have evidence of the familiarity of these artists with Japanese prints. Van Gogh's portrait of Père Tanguy, the print dealer, shows him against a background of Japanese prints, among which Hiroshiges and Kunisadas are prominent. He also painted an oil copy of a Hiroshige print, one of the 'One Hundred Views of Edo', with phoney calligraphy added on either side. In 1889 Gauguin painted his 'Still Life with a Japanese Print'. Gauguin's own landscapes are not in simple mimicry of the Japanese, but his colour orchestration shows how strongly the Japanese influence had worked on him.

Toulouse-Lautrec was less attracted to the landscapists than to the figure artists, but his debt to Utamaro, who by the 1880s was even rivalling Hokusai in popularity among Parisians, was great. From Utamaro he must have taken his assurance in posing single figures in splendid silhouette against a neutral background – the dominating outline of Aristide Bruant, for example, can be compared to the geisha O-hisa of Utamaro's print. Lautrec was naturally attracted to the *demi-monde* of Edo depicted by Utamaro, and he owned a copy of Utamaro's notorious erotic book *The Poem of the Pillow,* which he acquired from the Goncourt brothers, avid collectors of both Japanese prints and French contemporary posters. Lautrec's seal-like monogram, again copied from the Japanese, is more authentic than Whistler's. Of all Western artists, perhaps, Lautrec gained most from the discovery of Japan as an art force. With Vuillard, Bonnard, and de Feure, the debt is less to the Japanese print than to European variations on the print: just as, in the eighteenth century, 'chinoiserie' and 'japonaiserie' were based less on actual Chinese and Japanese silk and porcelain designs, than on the European 'vision of Cathay'.

Lautrec is the incontestable master of the colour lithograph poster: but Chéret was the pioneer. He was born in 1836, the son

Lautrec, second poster of Jane Avril, 1899. Initialled and dated in the plate.

opposite De Feure's poster for the Salon des Cent, Paris, 1894, has the delicate and passive quality of most of his work. The Japanese influence is very evident, even in the seal-signature.

of a journeyman typographer in Paris, and one of a large family. His father wanted him to train for some secure trade, as an iron-monger, a gardener, or chemist, but the boy was finally appren-ticed to a lithographer, and later to a printer, in whose workshop he designed menus, wedding cards, and funeral announcements. He found time to visit the Louvre and to attend classes at the Ecole des Beaux-Arts, where he was encouraged by Lecoq de Boisbaudran. He decided to go to London, but his first visit brought him no success. On his return to Paris in 1858, he was commissioned to design a poster for Offenbach's *Orphée aux Enfers*. He returned to London. This time he was commissioned to design a furniture catalogue for Maple's, and posters for a

ENTRÉE
0,50 cts

5me EXPOSITION
du 1er au 31 Octobre

SALON DES CENT · 31· Rue Bonaparte.

Imp. BOURGERIE & Cie, 83, Faubg St. Denis. Paris.

In this painting by Edouard Dammouse of his brother's pottery studio, 1899, one of Chéret's posters hangs on the wall, showing that Parisian contemporaries valued them as decoration.

circus troupe and for *David Copperfield*. As we have seen, he studied paintings by Turner, and learnt techniques of colour printing. His 1872 poster for the Bal Valentino brought him the patronage of Rimmel, the perfumer, who took him to Italy to study and then gave him the capital to start his own printing firm. The brightness and gaiety of his designs soon brought him many commissions, for anything from circuses to throat pastilles. To each commission, he applied the same techniques, the same kind of designs, and it is not possible to dismiss merely as misplaced patriotism the English critic Hiatt's verdict that 'To look at one of Chéret's posters is to look at them all'. Yet singly, they have marvellous vivacity and verve; as Edouard Dammouse's

1899 view of the interior of his brother's pottery studio shows, they were used as wall decoration as well as for advertisement outside. In Chéret's own studio, significantly, were photographs of pictures by Tiepolo and Fragonard, and sculptures by Rodin.

'Il n'est pas, de notre temps, d'artiste qui se soit emparé autant que M. Jules Chéret de l'affection du public, et l'ait aussi sûrement conquise,' wrote Maindron in 1896. (No contemporary artist has won the affection of the general public as unerringly as M. Jules Chéret.) Degas called him 'the Watteau of the streets'. Forain, in conversation with Degas, compared him with Tiepolo. Seurat tried, by adapting some of Chéret's figures in his paintings, to trap some of the posterist's prime quality of spontaneity, and formed a collection of Chéret posters. The carnival spirit of Chéret's designs had an intoxicating effect on young English students such as Dudley Hardy, who became, and (with rare but brilliant exceptions) remained, a poor man's Chéret. Having retired from poster work to what he had been taught to regard as the more dignified roles of oil painter, frescoist and pastel draughtsman, Chéret died, honoured by a museum of his works at Nice, in 1933. There is a particularly good account of Chéret's life in Lady Abdy's book *The French Poster: Chéret to Cappiello* (1969).

A delightful painting by Chocarne-Moreau, of 1894, illustrated in Crespelle's *La Belle Epoque* and in Lady Abdy's catalogue to the 1967 exhibition of Chéret's work at the Ferrers Gallery, London, shows a Chéret poster on an outside hoarding, torn and peeling. And it is worth noting what a fine arena for the display of posters Paris made at this time. When Chéret began printing posters, Napoleon III was demolishing the old narrow streets of Paris, and Haussmann was building wide ones with tall white buildings on either side. The far-apart walls were perfect sites for the new flamboyant posters. Again, as Mr James Laver has perceptively pointed out, in an introduction to *Nineteenth-century French Posters* (1944):

Paris lived in public. Many Parisians took all their meals, even the *petit déjeuner*, in one or other of the innumerable cafés which had sprung up everywhere. At the hour of the apéritif half the population was sitting at little tables on the pavement watching the other half go by.

England had not this advantage. Perhaps nothing could be more typical of the contrast between French and English life than the difference between the café and the public house. The 'pub' is an attempt to create a kind of cosiness, even, sometimes, a sphere of privacy. It looks inward towards the bar; the café looks outward towards the street. The café provides a row of *fauteuils d'orchestre*, and it was easy for the French artist to make himself the 'Mirror of the Passing World'. There was no need for the exoticism of the Romantics, or the Nature-study of the Barbizon school. His subject-matter was before him, a natural kaleidoscope providing him with an unending series of brilliant and exciting patterns. He had only to sit on a café seat and, when he got tired of that, to stroll over to the Moulin Rouge, or the Moulin de la Galette. For even when night had fallen, Paris continued to live in public.

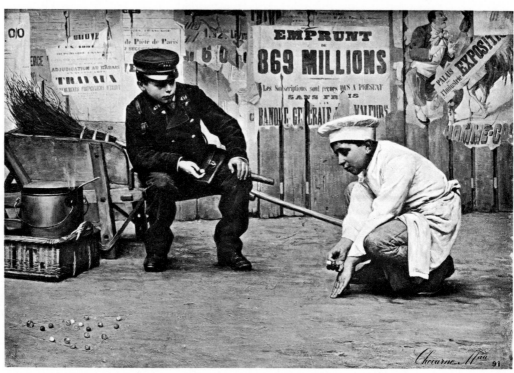

A further quotation, from *Confessions of a Young Man* (1886) – by that very impressionable and impressionist young man, George Moore – bears this out, and gives us a memorable idea of what it was like to be young in Paris when Chéret was in the first flight of his genius:

I did not go to either Oxford or Cambridge, but I went to the 'Nouvelle Athènes'. What is the 'Nouvelle Athènes'? He who would know anything of my life must know something of the academy of the fine arts. Not the official stupidity you read of in the daily papers, but the real French academy, the *café*. The 'Nouvelle Athènes' is a *café* on the Place Pigalle. Ah! the morning idlenesses and the long evenings when life was but a summer illusion, the grey moonlights on the Place where we used to stand on the pavements, the shutters clanging up behind us, loath to separate, thinking of what we had left unsaid, and how much better we might have enforced our arguments. Dead and scattered are all those who used to assemble there, and those years and our home, for it was our home, live only in a few pictures and a few pages of prose. The same old story, the vanquished only are victorious; and though unacknowledged, though unknown, the influence of the 'Nouvelle Athènes' is inveterate in the artistic thought of the nineteenth century.

How magnetic, intense, and vivid are these memories of youth! With what strange, almost unnatural clearness do I see and hear – see the white face of that *café*, the white nose of that block of houses, stretching up to the Place, between two streets. I can see down the incline of those two streets, and I know what shops are there; I can hear the glass door of the *café* grate on the sand as I open it. I can recall the smell of every hour. In the morning that of eggs frizzling in butter, the pungent cigarette, coffee and bad cognac; at five o'clock the fragrant odour of absinthe; and soon after the steaming soup ascends from the kitchen; and as the evening advances, the mingled smells of cigarettes, coffee, and weak beer. A partition, rising a few feet or more over the hats, separates the glass front from the main body of the *café*. The usual marble tables are there, and it is there we sat and aestheticized till two o'clock in the morning.

In the same book, Moore parrots many of the common artistic attitudes of the day, usually with a certain amount of naïveté mixed with hyperbole. For example, he says: 'In all sincerity I profess my readiness to decapitate all the Japanese in Japan and elsewhere, to save from destruction one drawing by Hokusai.' And when he first went to Paris, it was with the object of becoming a pupil of Cabanel: 'A satyr breaking through some branches carrying a woman in his arms had inspired an endless admiration, and his picture of Dante sitting on a bench under a wall reading to a frightened audience, increased my desire to identify myself with his vision; to feel the thrill of the girl's shoulder, as no doubt he had when she shrank back into her

top P.-C. Chocarne-Moreau, 'Le Petit Télégraphiste', 1894.

bottom P.-C. Chocarne-Moreau, 'La Partie de Billes', 1894.

Lautrec's poster of May Belfort, 1895.

opposite Henri de Toulouse-Lautrec: 'L'Artisan Moderne', 1894, a design for Niederkorn's art furnishings shop. The name 'Niederkorn' can be seen on the basket carried by the workman.

overleaf Lautrec's poster for Cycles Michael, signed with his monogram and dated 1896.

lover's protection, frightened by the poet's relation of what he had seen in hell.' So much for the *avant-garde* notions of the friend of Manet and Toulouse-Lautrec.

Even Lautrec submitted to the stern regimen of a conventional academic training in Paris. His master was the despised Bonnat, a facile and pedestrian painter, of whom his students sang:

Tu peins très bien la redingote,
Chacun sait ça,
Chacun sait ça,
Tu la détaches couleur de botte,
Sur fond caca,
Sur fond caca.

(You paint such lovely redingotes,
Everybody knows it,
Picked out in a shade just like old boots,
Against a background of shit.)

Lautrec wrote to his Uncle Charles in 1882:

> You may be wondering what kind of encouragement I am getting
> from Bonnat. He tells me: 'Your painting isn't bad, it's rather stylish
> ... but your drawing is quite frankly atrocious.' So I must pluck up
> courage and start again, when I've rubbed out all my drawings with
> bread crumbs.

Although he caricatured his master as a frowning, bearded
dominie towering over himself, a quaking little figure, cap in
hand, suggesting a certain amount of subterranean insolence,
Lautrec did in fact submit meekly to the discipline. Bonnat persuaded him to adopt a sombre palette, even got him to paint the
historical and mythological subjects which he had to master for
entry to the Ecole des Beaux Arts. Huisman and Dortu tell us:
'Lautrec, in spite of the gibes of his fellow students, was always
respectful of the craftsmanship of his teacher.' Yet, like a human-
ist obediently mumbling some inane catechism to keep his
teachers happy, Lautrec nursed his artistic heresies in private,
especially during the summer holidays in Languedoc, where he
painted horses, huntsmen and peasants with riotous colour and
brushwork bravura. Bonnat never understood Lautrec's work.
In 1905, as President of the Council of National Museums, he
declined an offer of a work by him to the Musée d'Art Moderne.

Lautrec left the Atelier Bonnat in 1889. He designed his first
poster two years later – the dramatic bill for the Moulin Rouge,
showing the gaudy figure of La Goulue, with the cruelly twisted
silhouette of Valentin le Désossé in front of her, and spectators,
in black, behind. When the Moulin Rouge had opened, in 1889,
Chéret had been commissioned to design a poster. A photograph
reproduced by Huisman and Dortu in their *Lautrec by Lautrec*
(1964) shows Lautrec with Tremolada, the assistant to Oller and
Zidler, directors of the Moulin Rouge, standing in front of two
copies of Chéret's poster. The difference between Chéret's Moulin
Rouge and Lautrec's is striking. Chéret is as appealing and pretty
as ever, with vivacious bare-back riders; Lautrec is powerful,
satirical – and honest. Francis Jourdain wrote:

> I still remember the shock I had when I first saw the Moulin Rouge
> poster at the foot of which a horizontal stroke joined the letter T to
> the first letter of the name Lautrec; I thought the signature read
> Hautrec. This remarkable and highly original poster was, I remember,
> carried along the Avenue de l'Opéra on a kind of small cart, and I
> was so enchanted that I walked alongside it on the pavement.

opposite Lautrec's poster for the
Divan Japonais, 1892.

In the next few years, Lautrec designed his greatest posters:
for the bawdy singer Aristide Bruant, with his long scarf; for
Jane Avril, whom he loved, the finest showing her at 'Le Divan
Japonais'; 'Confetti Bella'; 'Les Chaînes Simpson', and posters

Divan Japonais

75 rue des Martyrs

Ed Fournier
directeur

Hautec

for the 'two English Mays', May Belfort and May Milton. Sometimes his posters did not please his patrons, and the only success was *de scandale*. His sitters claimed he made them look grotesque – even Yvette Guilbert, whose looks he admired, preferred to commission a poster from Steinlen after Lautrec had warped her features, distended her mouth, emphasized her cheekbones, squashed her eyes into a bleary and lubricious smile. In 'Le Divan Japonais' she was shown decapitated, although instantly recognizable by those black-gloved, froggy arms that Lautrec had often sketched with a laconic mastery that even Hokusai could have envied.

The genius of Lautrec, coupled with his fame as a painter and the technicolor glamour of his strange life, has distracted attention from Théophile Alexandre Steinlen, who as a posterist has much in common with him. Steinlen was born in 1859, in Lausanne. He had an artistic background: his grandfather, Théophile Steinlen, was drawing master at Vevey, and many of his pictures are still there. (He had nine sons, of whom several were concerned with the arts, among others Aimé, who wrote the song 'Comme volent les années!', and Marcel, who did enamel work of remarkable fineness and designed the costumes for the *Fête des Vignerons* of 1865.) Steinlen did not enjoy his schooldays; but in his spare time he made drawings of animals, especially of cats. As a boy, he read Zola's *L'Assommoir*. It was a revelation to him, as to the young George Moore, the English *alter ego* of all progressive Frenchmen, and a near-contemporary of Steinlen. Moore wrote:

I had read a few chapters of the *Assommoir*, as it appeared in *La République des Lettres;* I had cried, 'ridiculous, abominable', only because it is characteristic of me to form an opinion instantly and assume at once a violent attitude. But now I bought up the back numbers of the *Voltaire*, and I looked forward to the weekly exposition of the new faith with febrile eagerness. The great zeal with which the new master continued his propaganda, and the marvellous way in which subjects the most diverse, passing events, political, social, religious, were caught up and turned into arguments for, or proof of, the truth of naturalism, astonished me wholly. The idea of a new art based on imagination, an art that should explain all things and embrace modern life in its entirety, in its endless ramifications, be, as it were, a new creed in a new civilization, filled me with wonder, and I stood dumb before the vastness of the conception, and the towering height of the ambition.

L'Assommoir turned more than one artist and writer away from academic artificiality in the direction of 'naturalism'. In Steinlen's case, the apocalyptic misery of the book, its world of travail and suffering, disgusted him with the petty-bourgeois life of Lausanne, its religious and social conventions. He decided that only among the *peuple affairé* of Paris would he be understood.

Portrait caricature of Steinlen by Uzès, published in *The Poster* of December, 1898.

overleaf Alphonse Mucha: poster for *Les Amants*, a comedy by M. Donnay at the Théâtre de la Renaissance, 1895.

But first he must complete his studies. He studied natural sciences at the Gymnase Classique of the Academy at Lausanne. He was encouraged in his art by three of the teachers. But studying for diplomas did not appeal to Steinlen, who drew more and more, beginning again ceaselessly, never satisfied. At twenty years old, after two years of university study, he was very unhappy. It was then that his sister wrote to one of his uncles, who placed him at Mulhouse with a manufacturing friend, to design textiles. He also copied on porcelain his grandfather's watercolours, and enjoyed his work. It was a delightful change from the slogging study at Lausanne. He found the robust observations of his fellow-workers a refreshing change from the bookish conversations of the university. But Mulhouse, too, was a small town; the country-side was dull and the people doggedly provincial. In 1881, Stein-len went to Paris – 'his eternal mirage', as his biographer puts it.

Through a friend, Bocion, the Lausannois painter, he found work in a textile-printing works, where he composed new designs of flowers and birds, to decorate handkerchiefs and fabrics for the Negro market. The head of the firm was so pleased with his work that he invited Steinlen to become his partner. Steinlen refused, wishing to stay independent. In the factories he worked at, he continually drew his fellow-workers. (Huysmans, too, had worked in a factory to get copy for his novel.) Beginning in an industrial art, he became an accomplished craftsman. His successive jobs meant that he never suffered from hunger; he could be generous to his art.

One day he was introduced by Willette, a designer friend who also became a well-known posterist, to the Montmartre cabaret of Rodolphe Salis, a great impresario who is reputed to have said: 'God created the world, Napoleon founded the Légion d'Honneur, and I have established Montmartre.' For Salis, Stein-len designed his magnificent poster advertising Salis's club, the

Self-portrait by Willette.

opposite A. Willette, 'La Revue Déshabillée, signed and dated in plate 1894.

LA REVUE DÉSHABILLÉE DE M. JEAN D'ARC. — TOUS LES SOIRS AU CONCERT DES AMBASSADEURS

COSTUMES DE M. WILLETTE

Théophile Steinlen, 'Lait pur de la Vingeanne, Stérilisé', 1894.

opposite Steinlen, 'Mothu et Doria', 1893.

'Chat Noir'. His next poster, for 'Lait pur Sterilisé de la Vingeanne' marks one of his few excursions into sentimentality: it shows his little daughter, Colette, with the inevitable cat. But Steinlen's great talent was for showing the poor of Paris as they were. If Lautrec's Montmartre is grotesque, distorted, full of theatrically wicked people, Steinlen shows us the Montmartre just outside the limelight. He had exactly the style of draughtsmanship needed to illustrate this sub-world – it has much in common with Van Gogh's strong and truculent handling. And the figures he so deftly sketches in are not troglodytish brutes, mindless urban peasants caught up in a cycle as inexorable as the changing of the seasons in the country; they are seen as individuals: the washer-woman shouting insults, the match-girl waiting in stolid silence as a toff fumbles in his pocket for change. Steinlen was a socialist,

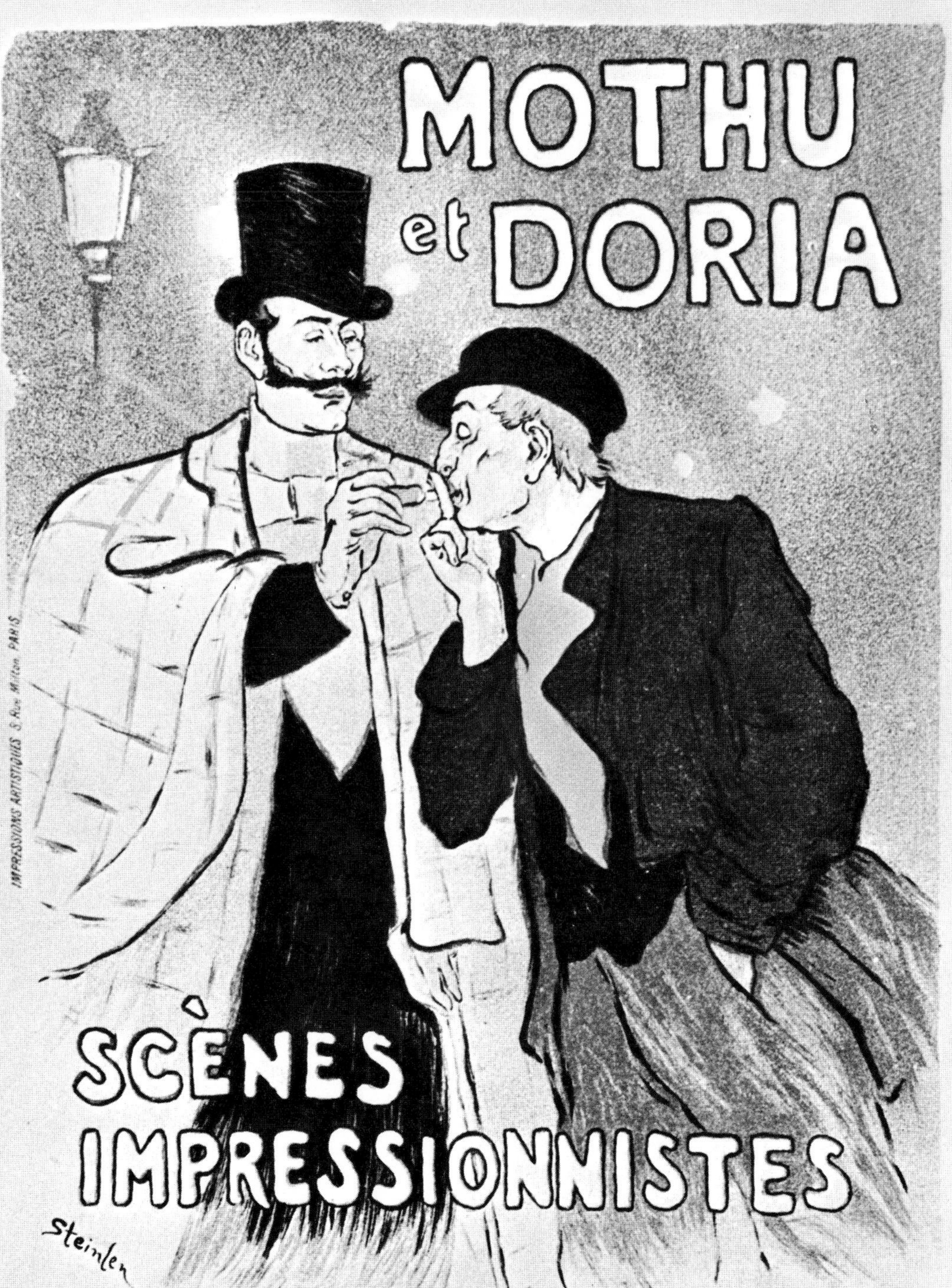
MOTHU
et DORIA
SCÈNES
IMPRESSIONNISTES
Steinlen

and there could be no better propaganda for his views than the quizzical regard of the top-hatted man, the resigned ironic expression of the *apache* in his superb poster for Mothu et Doria.

Alphonse Mucha was born within a year of Steinlen, in 1860; but from temperament and early training, his development as a posterist could not have been more different. Mucha was born in the town of Ivancice, South Moravia. He had a very religious childhood, for, with a good soprano voice, he was chosen as a chorister in the Roman Catholic baroque church, and later, at the convent of St Peter's, Brno. He saw much of embroidered copes, golden monstrances, rich plasterwork lit by wax candles, and his posters, designed to shout a message across the streets, still convey an air of antique ritualism, of muted choirs and dim, religious lights. In the Austro-Prussian War of 1866, the Prussian army occupied Ivancice, and Mucha's earliest cogent memory was of 'the last glorious pageant of ancient wars'. At Brno, he sang under the conducting of Leos Janaček (1854–1928), the composer. On a visit to Usti nad Orlici, he formed a rapturous admiration for the frescoes of Umlauf (1825–1916), the last representative of the Czech baroque tradition. Seeing Umlauf shuffling through the streets one day, Mucha realized that it was still possible, in the nineteenth century, to produce art which could challenge comparison with the masterpieces of the past.

Mucha became a theatre decorator and actor-producer. But when he applied to the Academy at Prague, with a view to extending his education in art, he was discouraged. In 1879, he answered a newspaper advertisement and went to Vienna as a painter with Kautsky-Brioschi-Burghardt, makers of theatrical scenery. But in December 1881, one of the largest Vienna theatres, the Ringtheater, was burnt down; the firm of Kautsky-Brioschi-Burghardt lost its best customer and had to dismiss some staff, including Mucha. He now became a freelance artist at Mikulov; his main work was designing tombstone inscriptions. Then Count Khuen, a local landowner, asked him to paint some frescoes in the dining room of his castle. He also sent him to his brother, Count Egon, who lived at Castle Gandegg in the Tyrol. An artist friend of the Count's told him that Mucha should study at the Munich Academy. He sat the examination in 1885, and was found mature enough to skip the first two years of training. In 1887, Count Khuen sent him to Paris for further study. There, as has been said, he worked under Lefèbvre, Boulanger and Laurens. He acquired the brilliant, refined draughtsmanship which again distinguishes him from the broad-working Steinlen, who was virtually self-taught. In 1889, Count Khuen's financial help was abruptly cut off. For some weeks, Mucha lived in poverty, hungry and ill. Then Henry Bourrelier, editor of the

opposite Will True, caricature of Alphonse Mucha, from *The Poster* magazine, November 1898.

opposite An anonymous and naïvely designed poster of the late 1890s, showing Bertoletti performing some of his tricks.

right Mucha's first poster for Sarah Bernhardt in *Gismonda*, 1894.

This design by Mucha for Waverley cycles
shows the complete assurance of his linear technique:
the composition is so deliberate as to be almost statuesque.

WAVERLEY

Petit Parisien Illustré, commissioned some illustrations. This was the year that Mucha first saw Japanese art, at the Paris World Exhibition. Like every influence he assimilated, that of the Japanese print was subtly adopted.

Mucha's first lithographs date from 1892, when he illustrated a calendar, published by Lorilleux, with pictures of children playing with signs of the zodiac, using figured frames for the text. This work brought him 2,500 francs and considerable publicity. It was the end of his hard times. Also in 1892, he produced a design for some lottery tickets – Bons de la Concorde – which for the first time give a suggestion of his characteristic future style, a mystical stylization already tending towards Art Nouveau. In this year, too, Armand Colin acknowledged his talent as a draughtsman and asked him to illustrate, with the academic painter Rochegrosse, a literary version of German history by Seignobos.

On St Stephen's Day, 26 December 1894, the manager of the Théâtre de la Renaissance asked M. de Brunhoff, director of the printing firm of Lemercier, if he could find someone to design a poster for Sarah Bernhardt's performance in Gismonda. Mucha happened to be at Lemercier's, correcting lithographic proofs, and Brunhoff sent him along to the theatre to make sketches. From these he made a full-length oil sketch for the poster. Brunhoff was frankly contemptuous, but when the sketch was shown to Bernhardt, she was delighted with it, and ordered the poster to be made. The lithographic work had to be done in such a rush that the upper part of the poster was not as finished as the lower. But it was printed and appeared on 31 December 1894. With its arresting design and soft pastel colours (Mucha eliminated from the finished work the touches of vermilion he had permitted in the oil sketch) it attracted crowds, and Bernhardt made a six-year contract with Mucha for the designs of her future posters and some of her stage sets and costumes.

Mucha's mature style has been so much identified with Art Nouveau that 'Style Mucha' has become another phrase for Art Nouveau in France, and the 1963 exhibition of his work organized by Mr Brian Reade at the Victoria and Albert Museum was entitled 'Alphonse Mucha and Art Nouveau'. It is possible to trace in Mucha's work the influence of the posterist Eugène Grasset, the decorative paintings of Hans Makart and the Japanese print: but the sudden dramatic flowering of his art into an extreme expression of Art Nouveau seems to have been a direct result of his encounter with Bernhardt, a living catalyst, and of his acute and sensitive observation of her performances. His famous poster for Job cigarette papers, with its wildly fantasticated pattern of curling hair strands and wafted cigarette

Eugène Grasset, design for
'L'Encre Marquet', 1892.

opposite Eugène Grasset, a poster for
the exhibition of his own work at the
Salon des Cent.

smoke, could easily, with a different slogan, be a poster for Bernhardt. Rumour, not substantiated, suggested a romantic liaison
between artist and actress: one newspaper even said she had
picked him up when he was riding in a wooden caravan through
Hungary. If there was not love – and there may have been –
there was certainly a strong sympathetic bond, one which
enabled Mucha always to represent the ideal Sarah, which was
the one she liked to see.

Allowing oneself a literary conceit, one might say that Chéret
was the springtime of the poster, with his fresh, insouciant
colours; Lautrec was its high summer; Steinlen, with his rough-

73

Mucha, poster for Job
cigarette papers, 1898.

opposite Lucien Fauré, poster for
Hurtu typewriters, 1897.

ness and brown-yellow tones, its autumn; and Mucha its winter,
snow mixed with every colour on the palette. None of the other
French posterists has the sustained distinction of these four,
although on occasion the others could produce exceptionally fine
designs: for example, Lucien Fauré's typewriter poster of which
the French version (whose name, 'Hurtu', had to be changed for
English sales promotion, as it suggested torture) was illustrated
in the first volume of *The Poster* magazine. De Feure at his best
has an Art Nouveau delicacy superior to Mucha's rather set,
stained-glass patterns. Bonnard's posters for 'France Champagne', the 'Salon des Cent' and 'La Revue Blanche' have an

74

Pierre Bonnard, 'Salon des Cent',
1896, signed and dated
in the plate.

opposite Lucien Métivet: 'Scala pour
vos beaux yeux', a signed poster of the
1890s for Emile Codey's revue.

icy fragility that none of the four great masters was quite dilettante or 'Japanese' enough to achieve, or even want. Lucien Métivet, a friend of Lautrec's, beat him in the competition held by the *Century Magazine*, New York, to advertise the *Life of Napoleon* that they were publishing (the judges included the academic painters Detaille and Gérôme, who probably found Métivet the less revolutionary). Adolphe Willette evidently thought Mucha too rarefied for poster work, as he drew a small girl kneeling before a Mucha poster as if it were the Virgin ('La pieuse erreur'); his own weakness was in draughtsmanship, although he designed some effective posters for *L'Enfant Prodigue* and *La Revue Déshabillée*, and a too effective anti-semitic poster for the *élections législatives* of September, 1889. Ibels, Grun, Forain and Anquetin were apt disciples of Lautrec.

In the twenty years 1880 to 1900, the poster was transformed from a vulgar disfigurement of the streets into an art form and even a collector's prey: at dead of night, the real fanatics would steal out with damp sponges to take the coveted Chéret or Lautrec off the walls. The poster also acted as one of the main carriers of 'that strange decorative disease', Art Nouveau. Before the 1880s, the poster had been modelled on, or only slightly adapted from, the academic painting; now the painters began to take their cue from the posterists.

opposite H. Ibels, poster for *Le Lever du Critique*.

Advertisement, in *The Poster* of July, 1898, for Edmond Sagot's poster shop, Paris.

iv. The Poster.—*Advertisements.*

ED. SAGOT.

39 bis rue de Châteaudun Paris

Artistic Posters

by the . .
Best Known Artists.

DRAWINGS.

LITHOGRAPHS.

ETCHINGS.

England to 1914

More strongly did he feel a distaste for Edwardian vulgarity. Vulgarity was the quality he disliked most; and he found the Edwardian brand especially unattractive. There was something aggressive and ungenial about it, as it manifested itself in Kipling's bullying militarism, in Wells's guttersnipe hostility to ancient culture, in the expensive grossness of Edward VII, in the new bustling commercialism that was defacing the country with advertisements.

The mention of 'vulgarity' at once suggests Henry James, who persecuted the vulgar as the Inquisition had persecuted heretics. But in fact the subject is Max Beerbohm, his attitudes here described by his biographer, Lord David Cecil. What must first strike the historian of the poster is the idea that Max regarded the hoardings – romantically viewed by certain Frenchmen as 'the art gallery of the boulevards' – as a degrading development to be classed with the other innovations he deplored. But more surprising, perhaps, is Max's impression that the Edwardian age *was* vulgar.

Younger men than him, Siegfried Sassoon, for example, Compton Mackenzie, L. E. Jones and Leonard Woolf, would look back on their Edwardian days as a serene, generous time: of pony-traps jogging down leafy lanes; of great hierarchies of servants, from the Admirable Crichton to the tweeny and skivvy; of trafficless roads, codes of honour, trailing dresses, croquet games and repressed scandals. In their accounts, the years before the outbreak of the Great War are the swansong, or, for the young, the last happy fling, of the English *ancien régime*. The idea is expressed in its extremest form by Derek Patmore, looking back to the London of 1909 in his autobiography *Private History* (1960):

It has lost some of the leisurely charm of its squares that were once bright with well-kept private houses, their gay awnings flaunting their colours against the green trees; and the parks have less of that opulence which was formerly typical of the prosperity of the British Empire. The people, too, looked so happy and confident – contrary to current ideas – for Britain still ruled the world and even the simple soldier in his scarlet uniform would feel that he belonged to a privileged race. Everything seemed so orderly. The traffic moved at a stately pace, and the whole of English life had the rhythm of a stately saraband. Life was still secure and confident, rigid in its social pattern and rather beautiful in its ordered grace. Like a beautiful building, it was a work of art and the result of centuries of civilization.

The picture of people walking about with fatuous smiles because they knew they had an Empire may seem a vision of cloud-cuckoo-land. But even Henry James, with his sensitive nose for vulgarity, felt the War as the tragic end of everything he had relished:

John Hassall, poster for Colman's Mustard, 1898. In spite of a broadly designed composition, the product itself is shown with photographic realism.

James broke off *The Ivory Tower* [wrote F. O. Matthiessen] because the modern age had sounded its first alarm in July, 1914. His sensitive antennae recorded at once an interpretation of what was happening. He had only a moment of shocked blankness that anything so 'infamous' could happen 'in an age that we have been living in and taking for our own as if it were of a high refinement of civilization'.

He died in February 1916: 'So here it is at last, the distinguished thing,' he murmured, welcoming the final negation of vulgarity and leaving behind the aptest possible monument to himself – an uncompleted Ivory Tower.

James could imagine the Edwardian age as 'a high refinement of civilization' by comparing it with the brash America he had escaped from. But Max, as a child of the 'nineties, a survivor, as he liked to put it, of the Beardsley era, applied to the new age the exacting aesthetic standards of a *fin-de-siècle* English exquisite, and found it horrible. The main change he noticed was that the glorification of femininity had given place to a 'strident admiration for mere maleness'. Could Kipling's name be a pseudonym for a female author, he asked: surely real men took masculinity more for granted. He detested Kipling's apparent admiration for the brute and the bully, the 'smell of blood, beer and baccy' which exhaled from his pages. The femininity run wild which Chéret and Toulouse-Lautrec had captured in their posters – frilled parasols, foaming can-can petticoats, embroidered fans, rococo conceits, boudoir diplomacy, the splatter of sunlight on springtime courtships beside the river – was replaced by a brass-band masculinity and by the formidable New Woman, suffragettes and the like. Max looked forward with foreboding to the day when there would be woman miners and 'steeple jills'. The Wilde scandal had put an end to the old Yellow-Book nonsense of floppy bow ties and hyacinthine locks. This was the age of the stiff upper lip. Men's collars became white manacles, and their hair was cropped with a penitentiary zeal. A ruthless music-hall bonhomie, with much reliance on the mock-cockney barrack-room slang popularized by Kipling, was now the common change of conversation.

The poster, with its glaring colours (pillar-box red, Reckitt's blue, Colman's yellow) was a natural vehicle for the art of this tough, gleefully vulgar time. And the two posterists who represented it most typically were John Hassall and his friend Dudley Hardy. They had similar temperaments. Heavily moustached, boozy and ribald, they had the air of officers recently risen from the ranks. (*The World* of 4 August 1914 said Hassall looked 'more like a soldier than an artist'.) On pier-ends they had their pictures taken together on the popular 'tin-types', sticking their beaming faces through pictures of ballet-dancers and nannies.

top John Hassall, *bottom* Dudley Hardy: 'On pier-ends they had their pictures taken together on the popular 'tin-types', sticking their beaming faces through pictures of ballet dancers.'

They rode about in pony gigs, sporting straw hats like those worn by Edwardian murderers and pork butchers in modern stage productions. They drank themselves silly in Paris cafés, sang in lusty baritones and roistered along the boulevards. Their life was one long *Diary of a Nobody* or *Three Men in a Boat,* full of jests and jolliness and hangovers. (Jerome K. Jerome was a friend and patron of both.)

Hassall is by nobody's standards a great artist. But he was, one might say, a hack of genius. The same prodigal flow of ideas as comes to the great artist or writer *malgré lui* came to him as well; but the ideas were translated into Hassall's bouncy, facetious style, and whatever subtle or sublime qualities might have been in them were sacrificed to obtain an effect of pawky humour. The lack of sensitivity apparent in his academic studies (those, for example, executed to a set subject in the beery Sketch Club meetings he was so fond of) was almost an asset to a poster-ist. As advertisements, his staring designs for Colman's Mustard or vacuum cleaners are superior to delicate fantasias such as Mucha's posters for Job cigarette papers, though, of course, they are below them considered as works of art.

John Hassall was born at Walmer in 1868. Educated first at Worthing, then at Newton Abbot College, Devon, he spent the last three years of his schooldays at Neuenheim College, Heidelberg. Returning to England, he decided to enter the army, but twice failed the examination for Sandhurst, and instead went to Manitoba to farm with his brother. Years later, in the days of his fame in England as 'the Poster King', he was asked by an interviewer from the boys' magazine *The Captain* (whose splendid cover he had designed) whether he had liked Manitoba. His reply could come straight from Jerome K. Jerome:

Not much, I didn't. Manitoba spells flies. Billions of 'em. You eat flies, drink flies, breathe flies in Manitoba, and it gets a little monotonous. I don't begrudge the time I spent there. It was an experience, and I have no doubt it did me good. One thing I have to thank Manitoba for, and that is, that the loneliness of the long winter evenings, and the lack of society, made me hunt about for something to occupy my time. A dozen sketches were the result.

His first artistic success came at the opening of an agricultural exhibition at Minnedosa, a small prairie town a hundred and forty miles west of Winnipeg – the nearest community to the Hassalls' farm. For the encouragement of prairie art three prizes were offered for the best pictures submitted. Hassall drove his into Minnedosa in a cart and carried off all three prizes, the highest being sixteen dollars. A year later another exhibition was held and Hassall again won all the prizes. On the approach of a

third exhibition, a deputation waited on him ('fingering their guns', as Hassall used to add in later versions of the story) and suggested that he should gracefully let the first prize go to the local Methodist parson's daughter and end the slump in native art. Hassall agreed, and 'clerical circles in Minnedosa were presently gratified by the news that their candidate had received the first award for a picture which the defeated candidate describes as "a fine study of a blue jay on a vermilion sky".'

Hassall now submitted some drawings of Christmas festivities to the editor of the *Daily Graphic.* They were accepted and appeared in the issue of 26 February 1890 – his first published work. He also sent some drawings to *Punch,* and the editor, Frank Burnand, had blocks made of them. One or two appeared, though several got no further than the proof stage.

But Mr Burnand must have thought they showed some promise, for he sent me a nice letter in which he compared my handling of the subject to Leech's – of course, very much to my disadvantage. He said Leech would have done so-and-so, whereas I had done just the opposite. He asked me to amend this particular sketch according to his instructions, which I did.

A friend with whom the Hassalls farmed suggested he should go in for drawing as a career. He returned to England and settled with his parents at Deal. After a few months making desultory sea sketches, he realized he was wasting his time without tuition. He went to see Sidney Cooper in Canterbury, but the old Academician was not impressed. Then someone told Hassall of a free school of art at Antwerp.

That was just my sort, so, in my usual haphazard way, I crossed to Antwerp and presented myself at the Academy there. They asked me if I had any sketches, and I said I had not. While they were trying to make me understand that they must have something in proof of my aptitude, and while I was trying to make them understand that any sketches I had were in England, an old man came along. He was evidently well-known there, and indeed, as I learned afterwards, was on a visit of inspection. He said, when he understood my grievance, 'You vill come to my studio, and in any months I vill make you to be an artist.'

The old man was P. van Havermaet ('Old Van'), a professor at the school, of which the director was the unpopular Albrecht De Vriendt. Hassall stayed there for six months, then went to Julian's in Paris where he studied for a further six months under Bouguereau and Ferrier. Then he returned to Antwerp for another spell of Bohemian student life. Cloaks were in; so were fancy dress charades such as that shown in a photograph of 1894. Hassall, always breezy and clubbable, fitted in well. *The Poster*

Two views of Hassall's studio in Kensington Park Road, London, *c.* 1900, showing poster designs amid the Oriental clutter.

of April 1899 described 'happy days spent in the Académie des Beaux-Arts and studios of Antwerp just five years ago', illustrating the article with two pictures of Hassall with his friends.

The accompanying photos were taken at the studio of 'Mynheer' Hassall, whose daily afternoon teas *met cookskies* were always a 'rendezvous' for all comers, and when amongst discussions artistic the possibilities of the 'Poster' were often brought forward ... The photo of Indians and Cowboys was taken shortly after the carnival of 1894, in which the English students played a prominent part, carrying off the second prize for the finest costumes. The costumes in this group are all 'home-made'.

The interviewer from *The Captain* throws light on the kind of work Hassall did at Antwerp:

'You didn't design posters at Antwerp, I guess?' said I, with a twinkle.
'Oh dear no,' replied Mr Hassall. 'I was going to be a great artist, of course. The kind of artist who paints enormous pictures, and gets infinitesimal prices for them, or fails to sell them at all. Yonder are two pictures I painted at Antwerp.'
Nearly the whole end of the studio was occupied with one of these, and the other, a smaller one, flanked it. They are both remarkable pictures, and so unlike the sort of thing which is associated with the name of Hassall today that I found it hard to believe that he painted them. He reached down the Royal Academy catalogue for 1895, and, lo and behold! there the two pictures were. One, entitled 'Birds of prey', represents a meeting of a gang of Nihilists, and the other, equally sombre both in treatment and subject, shows a despairing woman who is about to asphyxiate herself with charcoal fumes. Lively subjects these for the man who has brightened our dull streets with six hundred beautiful posters!

At this stage, Hassall seemed all set for instant success. His first drawings had been accepted by the *Graphic* and *Punch*; his first paintings, by the Royal Academy. But he could not afford to spend six more months on a painting, as he had on 'Birds of Prey'. He turned again to black-and-white work for immediate cash – 'and I can truthfully say that I was, metaphorically speaking, kicked out of every editorial office in London.'

It was now that Hassall discovered his most successful genre. The chance came with the receipt of a circular letter which David Allen and Sons, the colour-printers, had sent to several artists asking for designs for commercial placards. Could Hassall do posters? He thought he could, and called on Messrs Allen. Mutual enquiries as to what the artist could do and what the printers wanted resulted in Hassall's seizing a pencil and drawing on a scrap of paper the original design for the poster for 'The French Maid'. Allen's were quick to see Hassall's potential, and their association lasted for seven years, during which Allen's published some hundreds of Hassall posters. These included one of his most

opposite Hassall's most famous and longest-lasting poster, 'Skegness is *so* bracing', 1909.

G.N.R.

SKEGNESS
IS SO BRACING

successful designs, that for *The Only Way*. The *Captain* interviewer records:

Apropos of the well-known poster which advertized the play entitled *The Only Way*, Mr Hassall told me an amusing story. Mr Martin Harvey is represented going up the steps to the guillotine, while the Parisian mob is howling at the foot. The bootmaker's man came into the studio one day to take Mr Hassall's measure, and this particular poster seemed to exercise a weird fascination over him. The artist began to think what a thoughtful man this was, and how artistically impressionable. 'Ah, I see now!' the man exclaimed, the heavy clouds of thought lifting from his brow. 'I see now – the *only way* is up them there little steps!' And, as Mr Hassall remarked, 'He wasn't far wrong.'

Allen's also produced 'Poppy and her Trainer', the design that first made Hassall's name as a posterist. Most of his earliest posters were for the theatre; but with a request from Judson's, to design a poster for Moonlight Soap, he began a series of trade posters, including advertisements for Colman's Mustard, Nestlé's Milk, and the British Vacuum Cleaner Company. Johnson, Riddle and Company, who still use the (now adapted) presses on which Hassall's posters were printed, published some of his best designs advertising pantomimes, including Cinderella. They have recently produced some facsimiles, good enough to be confused with the originals.

Hassall founded a school of poster artists, as affectedly robust as the Beardsley school was affectedly decadent. His most prominent followers were Will Owen and Cecil Aldin, both his friends. Owen's style was so much like Hassall's that *The Times*, in its obituary of Hassall (9 March 1948) mistakenly credited him with Owen's 'Ah, Bisto!' poster ('His sympathy with children comes out in the engaging youngsters of the "Bisto" series of posters.') But Owen's poster is at least temporarily immortalized in the name of a recently established Hampstead restaurant: 'Ah, Bistro!' Hassall's most famous poster has also achieved an extra-mural after-life. The jolly fisherman of his 'Skegness is so Bracing' poster welcomes careful drivers into Skegness, and has actually been incorporated into the pendant of the mayoral chain of office. When Hassall died, the corporation sent a wreath in the form of the jolly fisherman.

The *Manchester Guardian* of 13 April 1934 reported:

Since then [1909, when Hassall designed the Skegness poster] no one has been able to say 'bracing' without thinking of Skegness ... All the caricaturists in Britain have used the poster at one time or another as a basis for their cartoons and comic men in the theatre have acted it.

To-day at Frascati's all this came to a head when the Skegness authorities and the L. and N.E. Railway gave a lunch to Mr Hassall

opposite John Hassall, poster for Veritas gas mantles. The 'Hassall dog' sits at the foot of the lamp-post, appealingly woeful.

John Hassall, proof before text of a design for Dobson, Molle and Co. Ltd, 1904.

and announced that they would put up a statue to him at Skegness where the clock tower now stands if he would design it himself. Meantime, a silver statuette of his jaunty fisherman was presented to him.

At the luncheon, Hassall explained how the idea for the poster had evolved. 'It had something to do with Romulus and Remus jumping over the little walls of Rome, and Skegness with its glorious air and sands making people jump without anything to jump over.' He denied that a former general manager of the railway had been the model for the design.

Hassall was also the originator of an animal character for which Cecil Aldin later got the credit. This was the mongrel dog, alternately impudent or woeful, used by Aldin in his merry public-house pictures and in a poster such as his 'Your Grandfathers drank Ellis Davies' Tea.' In *Pearson's Magazine*, 1900, the same creature is unequivocally described as the 'Hassall dog':

Every humorous artist has his favourite mascot with which he embellishes the greater part of his studies, and anyone who is at all familiar with John Hassall's work must of necessity have made the acquaintance of the mongrel dog who gives such a highly felicitous tone to many of his pictures ...

The proportions of the Hassall dog are singularly lank and ungraceful, delicately suggestive of a pedigree too complicated for words. His head is the most pronounced part of his composition, and is always touched into prominence by a highly intelligent countenance and eyes that speak of conflicting emotions. The like of this dog has never been seen in flesh and blood by any man, unless it be John Hassall, and he refrains from telling its whereabouts, but desires that it should go down to posterity known only as the 'Hassall dog'.

Hassall was twice married: first, in 1893, to Isobel Dingwell, by whom he had a son and two daughters; and secondly, in 1903, to Constance Maud, daughter of the Reverend A. Brooke Webb. The son of the second marriage was Christopher Hassall, the poet, dramatist, and biographer of Rupert Brooke; and the daughter is Miss Joan Hassall, whose delicate wood engravings are as far removed from her father's swashbuckling poster work as Ben Nicholson's abstracts are from the lovingly realistic still-lifes of his father, that other posterist, Sir William Nicholson (otherwise 'Mr W. Beggarstaff'.)

In his preface to an edition of Miss Hassall's wood engravings, Mr Ruari McLean vividly describes John Hassall's studio, in which she grew up:

A studio had been built out at the back of the house in the 1890s, occupying the whole garden, with a glass roof and high side-windows. When he died in 1948 the room had not been cleared for upwards of forty years. It contained a fantastic accumulation, for Hassall would throw nothing away which interested or amused him and seems to have had a wide circle of globe-travelling friends and family who always returned with presents to add to the collection. Surviving photographs show the artist at his easel against a grotto-like background, which includes early posters, statuettes, curios, masks, weapons, costumes, the ceremonial headdress of a Red Indian chief, suits of armour, and an Elizabethan four-poster bed. What looks like an ivy-covered wall turns out to be a collection of flags on pins from 1914–18 Flag Days, when that ingenious method of raising money from the public started. Among the objects discovered after John Hassall's death were a sprig of heather from Nellie Melba, a lump of raw copper from Captain Scott, and Napoleon's death-mask from John Tussaud. The dust that lay on the Indian gods and the ammonites was like grey sugar more than an inch thick.

Miss Hassall has kindly allowed me to reproduce some of the photographs mentioned by Mr McLean. She also allowed me to interview her in the manner of the newspaper reporter that I then was (would that it were possible to do the same with people who knew Toulouse-Lautrec!). What follows is based on that interview, of 30 April 1968.

Miss Hassall said that her father had 'a funny store of general knowledge', but she thought it would be fair to say he was uneducated. He knew nothing of literature or music, little even of art, beyond his own circle. He had a tendency towards tall stories: for example, he was one of the first into Wookey Hole, because he knew the owner; when he came home, the children eagerly asked what it was like. He said it was vast as St Paul's Cathedral, and when asked about the stalagmite known as the Witch of Wookey, he indicated something about six feet high. 'Years later,' Miss Hassall recalls, 'I went there myself. The place wasn't large at all – and as for the stalagmite, it was just like a little loaf on the floor.'

Hassall made a fine collection of ancient flints which he picked up at random on the seashore. It was eventually presented to the University of Cambridge, and Miss Hassall was with him at the opening of the collection.' The room was full of ageing professors, squabbling over microliths; but my poor father sat glowering in a corner: he didn't know the first thing about his own collection.'

'The trouble with my father was that he drank. He would come back after two or three days of absence with a bruised face and no account of where he had been.' I asked what led to the drinking. Miss Hassall thought there were four main causes. First, Hassall was a hopeless business man. He wrecked his own earning capacity by the amount he did for charity. Whole pages of his work books are headed 'Free' or 'Caritas'. In the First World War he got known as someone who would do something

Hassall at work in the Kensington
Park Road Studio, *c.* 1898.

Dudley Hardy in front of one of his
designs for *Today* magazine, 1899.

John Hassall, a poster protesting against the Sunday closing of public houses.

for nothing (one of the photographs shows him sketching for war charities in Trafalgar Square). And he was diddled, too – by his printers, and by one MP who ordered two huge canvases and never paid for them. Secondly, there was Hassall's unhappy second marriage:

> Mother came from a country vicarage, and she brought her vicarage mind with her. She disapproved of my father's friends, who were a Bohemian, beery lot. And I think she had been brought up to think sex was something rather wicked. When my father got drunk, or got into debt, or wouldn't wear spectacles, she didn't do anything. She just went to church and prayed a little harder.

Thirdly, he was partly broken down by an experience in the Great War. He had been sworn in as a special constable. One day he had to go to the scene of a munitions factory disaster 'to pick up the pieces'. Miss Hassall said her mother had told her he used to wake up crying for weeks afterwards. 'It altered his whole attitude to life.' Finally, he suffered from failing eyesight. Immoderately vain of his appearance (hence the many photographs of him), he wouldn't wear spectacles. When urged to do so, his stock reply was: 'I tried on old so-and-so's at the Sketch Club, and they were no good at all.' He used a magnifying glass: but the standard of his work declined, and he became more depressed. He got very eccentric. Though he had splashed the hoardings with violent colour, he came to loathe anything bright or light – 'out of tune', he would call it. Letters had to be kept under cover. When his wife went on holiday, she returned to find that the drawing room had been painted chocolate brown. Hassall also ruined some fine first editions by painting their spines brown.

'He was full of invention and strange ingenuity.' He built a false door leading from his studio into a little workroom. It was in the form of a simulated bookcase, and one volume of a mock encyclopedia was labelled 'BAC to BIZ'. He painted eggshells to look like comic figures. His posters were full of fairy people in medieval costume, with huge bedroom slippers and tall hats. Miss Hassall said of the women's two-horned headdresses: 'if you try to make one, as we once did to go to a fancy-dress ball, you can't.' Hassall always 'made' the face he was drawing, by grinning, frowning, or leering horribly into a looking-glass. Bruce Bairnsfather, one of his pupils, based his famous character 'Old Bill' ('If you knows of a better 'ole, go to it!') on Hassall.

Flipping over the pages of one of Hassall's work books (most of his other papers have been given to the University of Essex), we came across an entry recording a poster for Borwick's Baking Powder. Miss Hassall recalled: 'They asked him to do them a poster with the caption "Will you let us help you to rise?" He was given the commission at Easter; the poster he designed was returned as "blasphemous".'

Dudley Hardy should by rights come before Hassall in a history of the poster, for he really introduced the colour poster into England with his 'Yellow Girl' for *Today* magazine. But he is a less considerable figure. His posters are strongly derivative of Chéret's: it would not be unfair to call him the poor man's Chéret. Like Chéret, he appreciated the advertising value of sex-appeal, and his recurring subjects are legs, tu-tus, frou-frous, and legs again. The range of expression and antic is between a frisky insouciance and a brassy glamour – for the design of Alhambra coryphées, this was the acceptable counterpart to the bluff Kiplingesque male.

He was born in 1867, in Sheffield, son of the marine painter T. B. Hardy: 'I was born with a brush in my mouth,' he liked to say. His boyhood was spent in his father's studio. At fifteen he was sent to the Academy at Düsseldorf, where he studied under Crola and Löwenstein, but the regimen seemed harsh after the freedom of his father's studio. Eventually he mutinied and was dismissed. He stayed in Düsseldorf for a while and worked from nature – landscapes and character studies. A number of these studies was bought by an American visitor for £40. But like Hassall, he reached the stage where he felt the need of some academic discipline. He returned to the Academy and was magnanimously readmitted after showing samples of his work. After three months there, he came home. He worked in his father's studio and then under A. A. Calderon. Later he went abroad again, this time to Antwerp, where he put himself under Verlat. At this time he had to turn to hack-work for money. He became a master of the pot-boiler: later, while living in London, he acted as 'a war artist in the Soudan' for a journal. His pictures for this, it was said, 'verily reeked of the smoke of battle'.

He was offered black-and-white work on another paper, but refused and went to Paris to study under Raphael Collin and Carl Rossi for two years. Then he returned to London to settle down, and became a member of the Royal Society of British Artists. Already he had exhibited in London with success. His first picture to be hung in the Academy was shown in 1885, when he was only eighteen. In the next year he exhibited 'The Angelus', and in 1888 'The Nomads' was hung on the line and bought at the private view. His Paris pictures were exhibited at the Suffolk Street gallery of the RBA. One of them was 'A la Foire', a scene at a French suburban fair which can be seen in A. E. Johnson's 1909 book on Hardy. It shows that he had taken to heart the lessons to be learnt in Paris.

opposite Dudley Hardy: original design for a Bertram Mills Circus poster, 1920. It shows Hardy at his very best, and is owned by Peter Blake, the 'pop' artist, whose style has something in common with Hardy's in its use of flat but brilliant colours.

His first large canvas also dates from 1888. 'Sans Asile' made his reputation. Shown at the Paris Salon, and later at Munich, Düsseldorf and Berlin, it was bought by the City of Sheffield. It is a badly painted, ill-composed scene of homeless men dossing by one of the lions in Trafalgar Square. In 1892 he painted another famous work, 'The Moors in Spain', full of voluptuous colour. It is now in Venice. Like so many artists of his time – and originality was not Hardy's forte – he painted Moorish scenes, Breton studies of peasants and seafolk. Only in his really brilliant draughtsmanship did he manage to find release from the repressive academic conventions of the day. The pages reproduced here, from two of his sketchbooks, are marvellously spirited – almost in the Phil May class – and they illustrate perfectly the social attitudes of Hardy, Hassall and their circle. A raw-handed, gap-toothed maid ('To the amusement of Celestine'); a straw-sucking bumpkin winking at a proper young miss in her waist-strangling corsetry; a representative of the 'New Woman', dressed in cycling gear and smoking: these were all stock characters from the doggedly limited *comédie humaine* they insisted on making of life. At the same time, two of the sketches show Hardy adventuring into a novel, laconic statement, light with Art Nouveau feeling, which goes beyond Phil May into the intellectual doodle-world of Gaudier-Brezska or Munch. Thickened, like a hair hung in alum solution to form crystals, this expressive line of Hardy's made him an effective advertiser.

Hardy's first poster was for one of Sir Augustus Harris's theatrical ventures, and another bill, for 'A Gaiety Girl', had helped to make that play popular. During the run of the 'Gaiety Girl', the theatre was decorated with a frieze of the posters. But his first great success, the poster that was later seen as the origin of the 'poster craze' in England, was an advertisement for Jerome K. Jerome's monthly magazine *Today*. Jerome wanted a placard for the paper which would 'have TO-DAY writ large upon it, metaphorically as well as actually'. Hardy's 'Yellow Girl' poster was the result, an outrageously chic girl in a flaunting mustard costume, holding a walking stick behind her shoulders. A. E. Johnson wrote:

The effect was startling, and no advertisement ever achieved its purpose more simply or more completely. The Yellow Girl refused to be ignored. There was something almost immodest in the way she danced, with mincing steps, along the decorous streets of London. She was irresistible, and the most solemn old sobersides that ever wore elastic boots found himself arrested and compelled to stare rudely at her ... The Yellow Girl took the town by storm.

Three drawings from Dudley Hardy's sketch-books:
'they illustrate perfectly the social attitudes
of Hardy, Hassall, and their circle.'

opposite Dudley Hardy's sketch for his 'Gaiety Girl' poster, 1894.
above The finished design, which owes much to Chéret in style.

Like most of Hardy's posters, the Yellow Girl reminds one forcibly of Chéret. *The Poster* magazine of October, 1898, with the chauvinism of its day, could suggest that Hardy was a better posterist than Chéret, because more varied:

Chéret is a king in his own particular line, but that line *is* particular, and unfortunately the platitude that when one has seen one of Chéret's, one has seen all, is perfectly true. The subject may alter slightly, the treatment and composition practically never, and it speaks volumes for the extraordinary artistic quality of his work, that it should still be in constant demand. It is in this that Dudley Hardy's strength lies. He is never monotonous. A new poster of his is always sought for with interest, as everyone knows that something fresh will be found. Each poster strikes a distinct note in itself. The refined sauciness of the 'Yellow Girl', and the wild abandon of the 'Gaiety' one, the queenly grace of 'Cinderella', the dignity of the 'Chieftain', the comical pathos of 'Oh! Susannah' and the comfortable prosperity of the 'J. P.'.

This is a piece of obvious special pleading, and as far as Chéret's reputation is concerned, no one could seriously entertain it now. But the claim made for Hardy's variety of invention is fair enough. It is at its best in the series of posters he designed for the Savoy operas of Gilbert and Sullivan staged by D'Oyley Carte. The first of these was for 'The Chieftain', by Sullivan and Frank Burnand: a flamboyant figure with a long stick and black ribboned hat against a background of glowing red. Hardy regarded it as his best poster. The monolithic white writing which formed an irregular line across the whole design could be read from a long distance. There followed 'The Grand Duchess', in white, green, red and chocolate brown: *The Poster* commented in March 1899, 'The very noble dame whose prodigious train is borne by two little niggers in livery is a quite majestic figure, obviously patrician to her finger-tips.' 'The Grand Duke' was a companion study. 'The Yeomen of the Guard' was advertised by a masked headsman with axe and block, and here *The Poster* severely wondered 'whether an opera, which, in spite of occasional lapses into genuine pathos, is on the whole light and amusing, was altogether properly announced by so severe and repellent a design.' Further Savoy posters included 'His Majesty' (the design inspired by a pack of playing cards); 'The Rose of Persia'; 'Oh! Susannah!' (with Louie Freear); 'The Geisha' (with Marie Tempest); 'The Lucky Star'; and 'Cinderella'. In 'The J. P.' he originated the much imitated device of setting the figure against a solid black background with only face and hands, collar, tie, cuffs, shirt and the highlights on boots, showing.

The posters of Chéret and Toulouse-Lautrec have the same relation to grand art as the Japanese woodcut prints which so

largely inspired them: widely regarded in their day as attractive and naughty ephemera of the *demi-monde des beaux arts* (to the Japanese, the Ukiyo-e, or 'Floating World'), they had qualities which came to be prized far beyond those of the laborious paintings of academicians. Similarly, one might say of Hardy's posters, that they had the same relation to mainstream English art of the period, as Gilbert and Sullivan's Savoy operas had to serious music: vulgar, amusing, popular, and with qualities that have ensured their survival while more self-consciously 'classical' works are disregarded.

One contemporary judgment which time has confirmed is that the Beggarstaff Brothers were the finest English posterists of this period. What they achieved was both revolutionary and peculiarly English, and its influence is still evident today. William Nicholson and James Pryde were not brothers, although they became brothers-in-law. In an article called 'Arcades Ambo: The Beggarstaff Brothers at Home', published in *The Idler* of 1895, an anonymous interviewer asked the two young men, then living in a house near Uxbridge, why they had chosen the name. It had, apparently, nothing to do with Dean Swift's pseudonym of Isaac Bickerstaffe (Evelyn Waugh in his autobiography *A Little Learning* mistakenly wrote that the 'Bickerstaff' brothers were among his favourite artists when he was at Oxford in the 1920s). In fact, they had found the name in an old stable, on a sack of fodder. 'It is a good, hearty, old English name, and it appealed to us; so we adopted it immediately.'

In later years, Nicholson and Pryde grew apart, and there was even some bad feeling between them, partly caused by Pryde's jealousy over Nicholson's establishment success and eventual knighthood. Max Beerbohm, in one of his series of cartoons, 'The Old and Young Selves', maliciously showed the two of them looking back at a sort of Siamese twin formed of both of them. 'Who were that?' asks Nicholson. 'Who was those?' asks Pryde.

Pryde was born in Edinburgh in 1866, the son of Dr David Pryde who since 1863 had been lecturer in English literature at the Edinburgh School of Arts. He became a student at the Royal Scottish Academy School, where W. M. Frazer and D. Y. Cameron were among his contemporaries. He went to Paris and, like Hassall, studied under Bouguereau. On his return, he came to London. His sister Mabel had persuaded her parents, when she was about seventeen, to let her study art at Hubert von Herkomer's school in Bushey. Max Beerbohm said she looked like 'the result of an intrigue between Milton and the Mona Lisa', but she attracted William Nicholson, the youngest of the boy students at Herkomer's, and after her first term there, they

A cartoon of the Beggarstaff Brothers by Will True, published in *The Poster* of 4 July, 1898. William Nicholson is the shorter figure on the left, James Pryde the taller on the right.

became engaged. For a time, James Pryde shared lodgings with his sister at Bushey, and naturally came to know Nicholson well. Not a student at Herkomer's himself, Pryde was a subversive influence outside, making clear his contempt for the dingy academicism taught in the school. In 1890 he exhibited a pastel of his landlady's daughter, Miss Mutton, under the more romantic title 'The Little Girl in Black', at the Grosvenor Gallery. It was favourably noticed by the critics. Nicholson, who was given the drawing, was now strongly influenced by Pryde. For a similar 'piece of Whistlerian impudence' he was expelled by Herkomer. In 1893, Mabel Pryde married Nicholson, and a year later their eldest son, Ben, was born.

In 1893, Nicholson was only 21. He was born at Newark-on-Trent, the son of William Newzam Nicholson, M.P., who had married Elizabeth Prior of Chaucer's House, Woodstock. He was educated at the Magnus School, Newark, and received his earliest artistic training from William H. Cubley of that town, who had been a pupil of Sir William Beechey, R.A., the pupil of Sir Joshua Reynolds. Later he too went on to Paris, to study at Julian's, where Bonnard and Vuillard, as well as Pryde, had been students before him. It was on his return that he became Herkomer's pupil.

William and Mabel Nicholson set up house in 1893 at the Eight Bells, Denham, near Uxbridge, a small eighteenth-century cottage (illustrated at the beginning of *The Idler* article) which had previously been a public house. Pryde became a frequent guest, and their collaboration as posterists began at this time. Pryde describes the evolution of the Beggarstaff poster in an autobiographical fragment quoted by Mr Derek Hudson in his biography of Pryde:

At that time posters in England were, with two or three exceptions, anything but striking, although there were some very interesting poster artists working in Paris. For example, Chéret, who did some notable work for the 'Divan Japonais', and de Toulouse-Lautrec who in addition to *affiches* for the same *café chantant* did some remarkable designs of Yvette Guilbert, Jane Avril, Caudieux, and others.

Poster art in England was just being redeemed by Dudley Hardy, whose *Yellow Girl* for the Gaiety Theatre [*sic*] was a clever piece of work; Maurice Greiffenhagen, later a Royal Academician, who did a poster for the *Pall Mall Budget*; and Frederick Walker, whose *Woman in White* really looked like an enlarged reproduction of a black-and-white drawing of his own. There was also Aubrey Beardsley's poster for what was then regarded as the advanced theatre in London, the Avenue. This last found little favour in the eyes of *Punch*, which, referring to it, made the suggestion 'Ave a new poster'. These were oases in the desert of others designed by regular workers for various firms.

Maurice Greiffenhagen, poster for the *Pall Mall Budget*, 1893.

This was the condition of affairs when I decided to become a poster artist. The statement is incorrect. I should rather say when I decided to become half a poster artist. The other half was, of course, my brother-in-law, William Nicholson, who lived in Denham, Bucks. One day, when we were together, a friend told us he had heard there was going to be an exhibition of posters at the Westminster Aquarium, and we thought we would like to do some for it. Nicholson asked me to go to the country and collaborate with him in these posters ...

For the exhibition we did five or six large designs, not for any particular firm's commodity but merely for a given article to which the firm's name could be applied. Thus, we did a design for pianos, another for niggers, and so on. We made them fairly large, for some were twelve feet high ...

We decided that a silhouette treatment was the best, and it had this advantage, that it had not been done before. Moreover, it was a very economical way of producing a poster for reproduction, for the tones were all flat. To get this flat effect, we cut out the designs in coloured paper and pasted them on flat boards or paper. Tom Browne, the black-and-white artist, who was working for a printer in Nottingham at the time, told me of his delight in finding that the method was so easy to reproduce.

After the exhibition, Nicholson and I took to doing posters for actual firms on approval. We would take the design under our arms and call on the people to whom we desired to show them, but I must confess our success was small. Our appearance with these enormous rolls of paper was made the subject of a drawing by Phil May, the original pencil sketch of which I treasure, but he omitted the roll in the finished black-and-white drawing which was eventually published.

Among the tragedies of that time which, happily, we can now laugh at as comedies, was the poster of a Beefeater – a suggestive design printed in three colours, red, black and yellow, which we thought particularly appropriate for a beef extract. We took it to the office of the firm in question and pinned it up on the wall of the very small room into which we were shown. After a while, the art editor or manager or whatever he called himself, a dear old gentleman rather like Father Christmas in appearance, came into the room; he gave the poster one glance and went out of the room without saying anything. Later, it was offered to Sir George Alexander, who had a Beefeater on the hoardings of the St. James's Theatre, but he did not find it suitable. Still later, that poster was redeemed by the proprietors of *Harper's Magazine*, who reproduced it freely in the United States, where it had a great success in advertising that publication, and it also had a vogue here for the same purpose.

Sir, then Mr Henry Irving asked us to do a poster for him for the one-act play *Don Quixote* which he was then about to produce at the Lyceum. It represented that character on a white horse with his long lance in hand and a windmill in the background. He bought it, but it never appeared on the hoardings, for the play failed and was soon withdrawn.

When, subsequently, Irving was going to produce *Robespierre*, Miss

Beggarstaff Brothers, poster for
Rowntree's Elect Cocoa, 1900.

Ellen Terry suggested we should design a poster for it and she would
show it to him. Miss Terry broke the news that Nicholson and I
intended to take a design to show him. He shook his head mournfully
and exclaimed: 'No more mills'. He never looked at our design.

Although we had started as the Beggarstaff Brothers, we soon
omitted the 'Brothers' and signed our work simply 'Beggarstaffs', the
form in which most of the reproductions appeared. When we had
attracted sufficient notice, a firm, the Artistic Supply Company,
Limited, asked if we would design posters and let them submit them to
various firms with a view to obtaining orders. On their suggestion, we
designed a poster for Messrs Rowntree's Elect Cocoa which was accepted and duly appeared on the hoardings. Then they suggested
we should do one for the forthcoming Drury Lane pantomime of
Cinderella. During the rehearsal of the pantomime the Supply Company took it to Drury Lane and it was hung up on the stage, where it
was made the subject of several jests by the comedians, one of whom
was Dan Leno. It was likewise regarded by Sir Augustus Harris as
something in the nature of a joke.

While it was hung up, Phil May happened to stroll on to the stage
during a rehearsal, saw it, and went up to Gus Harris and congrat-
ulated him on his acumen in having secured it. The result was that
Harris immediately accepted it and placed it on the hoardings. It was
simply a coach in a flat red colour with the head of Cinderella with
golden hair and black palings, with the word 'Cinderella' with the
lettering very clear and readable. I think the poster had a distinct
success.

The Beggarstaffs showed four designs at the Westminster
Aquarium in 1894, for 'Nobody's Candles', 'Nobody's Washing
Blue', 'Nobody's Pianos', and 'Nobody's Nigger Minstrels'.
In his book *Picture Posters*, Charles Hiatt wrote: 'If each
"Nobody" is not rapidly converted into "Somebody" the various
manufacturers and proprietors of the articles mentioned above
must be very stupid people. All were excellent; that which
advertised Nobody's Pianos was a most curious and a most
original performance.' But the designs were never used.

The first Beggarstaff poster to appear in the streets was a
design for *Hamlet*, a stencil made for Gordon Craig, who had
just joined a touring company. *Hamlet* was to open in Hereford
in September 1894, and Nicholson and Pryde began work on the
poster in July. It showed Craig as Hamlet, in profile and holding
a skull. Every copy was stencilled by hand in the Denham cottage, and the copies were posted in Hereford before the end of
August. The Hamlet poster is signed 'J.W. Beggarstaff, Denham,
Uxbridge', and the same signature appeared on their next poster,
of October, 1894, for 'Kassama' cornflour, commissioned by
Henderson's of Glasgow. Most of their subsequent posters were
signed 'Beggarstaffs'. Before the end of 1895, they had finished

Beggarstaff Brothers, poster for the
one-act play *Don Quixote* which was
produced by Henry Irving at the
Lyceum, 1896.

'A Trip to Chinatown' (marred by borders and lettering added by the printers without consulting the artists); the Beefeater, the design for Rowntree's Cocoa, the Don Quixote, and the Cinderella. In this period, too, they designed the 'Roundhead on Horseback', never used, but illustrated for the first time in *The Poster* of February, 1899; a cover for *The Hour*, and 'Girl on the Sofa', commissioned by Macmillan's but rejected (it was, however, probably the inspiration for Beardsley's design for one of Leonard Smithers's book catalogues).

They also prepared a poster for Irving's *Becket*, but this too was never used. Mr Derek Hudson points out that it is referred to by Gordon Craig's mother, Ellen Terry, in her manuscript notes on a copy of a book by Pryde's father, *The Highways of Literature*, now in the British Museum: 'The dear old David Pryde who made this book, & gave it me, is the Father of a great Artist – *James* Pryde – who, amongst other wonderful work, made a Poster of Henry Irving as "Becket", & gave it me, as H——— I——— could not, (for some reason unknown to any of us –) see his way to publish it. – E.T.' The poster is reproduced in Charles Hiatt's book of 1895. The Beggarstaffs also designed a poster for the Black and White Gallery (a reproduction is in the Victoria and Albert Museum) and a lost signboard for the Goat Tavern, Kensington.

How did the Beggarstaffs' collaboration work? On one level, Nicholson was the more businesslike of the two. Edward Gordon Craig, whose own style owed so much to the tuition of Pryde, wrote to Mr Hudson:

I knew J. P. and W. N. P. N. (whom we called 'The Kid') when they were inseparable – always together in life and work – J. P. without the faintest notion (or shall we say *wish* to learn) about business – or what it mattered – and N. quite practical, adroit, and damned if he'd become an unknown artist while Beardsley, Conder, Max B. and a whole Yellow Book of Artists had become celebrated in a night. And thanks to his practicality, J. P. lived, ate, drank (and didn't gamble) and developed a worth-while personality. One can *not* forget or make little of this fact – Pryde really might have died but for Nicholson.

On the other level, of their artistic coalition, it is difficult to assess the contribution of each. Pryde's champions would point out that he was quite capable of designing the fine advertisement for Nairn's Inlaid Linoleum, and the cover design for *The Poster* in 1899 on his own. They point, also, to his great dusky interiors, including the oil-painting of a towering bed which enabled Max to call him 'a specialist in posters and four-posters', and they suggest that Pryde must have contributed the dramatic element so essential in poster design. Nicholson's defenders, on the other

James Pryde, cover for *The Poster* of February, 1899.
This solo performance indicates how much of the
Beggarstaffs' genius was contributed by Pryde.

hand, refer to his books of woodcut designs, including the impression of Queen Victoria with her dog which became as canonical as Arthur Rackham's of Edward VII in *Peter Pan in Kensington Gardens*. Here, they suggest, was the genius of the association, with his unerring black outline. The only help the *Idler* interviewer is able to give on this point is that 'their methods seem to be so dovetailed in from beginning to finish, from the conception of an idea to its final expression, that we could learn nothing more exact as to their differences of feeling, than that Pryde generally uses a penknife to cut out the masses of coloured paper which form their original designs, while Nicholson employs a pair of scissors.'

A writer with the initials of R. M. contributed some verses to the *Westminster Gazette* of 13 January 1899. 'The Blind Beggarstaff of Bethnal Green' is a threnody for a Beggarstaff poster ('Rowntree's Elect Cocoa') blotted out by a Bass advertisement:

A splotch of mud on a Beggarstaff Man,
A splotch and that is all:
But it blinds the eye of the Cocoa Man
On a Bethnal Green dead wall . . .

O face with an eye that is all obscured,
O Master whose work is done,
'Tis best that thou at last art blind,
O Pride of a Nicholson . . .

The paste-pot fiend from his ladder leans,
Craned o'er like a young giraffe,
But, courage, Man with the darkened orb,
Lean on thy beggar's staff . . .

O cocoa man . . . thy sands are run,
Thy day draws dark. Alas!
The paste-pot churl in sections brings
The label of the Bass.

And o'er the splotch that shatters thine eye,
A yellow-red sheet is spread;
O Cocoa Man of the fine few tints,
Though buried, thou art not dead.

It was true. Posterists like McKnight Kauffer, thirty years later, would acknowledge the supremacy of the Beggarstaffs among their English precursors, and the influence they had had on them. And in the poster revival of the 1960s, Beggarstaff lettering was seen on the hoardings again. Contemporary artists admired them too, but did not quite understand. Mainly this was because of the different influences other artists had accepted. For example, Dudley Hardy told Percy Bradshaw, author of *The Art of The*

MENU.

Phil May, poster for the Booksellers'
Trade Dinner of 1895.

opposite Original sketch by Dudley
Hardy for the Playgoers' Club Dinner
of 12 January 1905. Edward Gordon
Craig is the central figure; behind him,
Hardy has parodied the Beggarstaffs'
poster for *Hamlet*.

Illustrator, that the main influences on him had been Josef
Israels, Henner, Mesdag, Fortuny, Jan van Beers, Chéret and
Willette. There is a dominance of the Dutch realist school. But
the Beggarstaffs told the *Idler* interviewer: 'One man we admire,
and that is Lautrec. He is one of the few artists who understand
what a poster is and should be.' They added: 'There is one thing
you mustn't forget to mention, and that is the great help we have
received from dear old Phil May, one of the kindest and best
friends we have had throughout.' Phil May was not, of course,
primarily a posterist, but a 'black-and-white man'. His contribution to the Beggarstaffs' thinking was the economy of his line.
A writer in the *Daily Chronicle* of 16 June 1904, describing
some of Phil May's early work for the *Sydney Bulletin*, recalls

EXHIBITION OF 150 DRAWINGS BY PHIL MAY.

NOW OPEN AT THE

FINE ART SOCIETY'S 148 NEW BOND STREET.

his reply to the editor who asked him to 'finish up' his drawings a bit. 'When I can leave out half the lines I now use,' May said, 'I'll want six times the money.' May also helped to spread an interest in the great French posterists: a photograph in *The Poster* of January, 1900, shows him in his studio in Holland Park Road, London, with Chéret posters (including that for the Musée Grévin) on the walls.

In the *Poster* photograph, May is shown, in this very 'artistic' setting, in riding dress. *The Review of Reviews* of 20 August 1903 reported:

His fondness for picturing himself in horsey costume led to a misconception of his character, and he remarked to an interviewer: 'By the way, I believe that some people imagine that I am a dare-devil sporting man. I don't so much mind the application of the first part of the phrase, but I am not a betting man, and have never been to a race meeting in my life, except on one or two occasions, when I went on behalf of a paper.'

But Cecil Aldin, the posterist and draughtsman already briefly mentioned, did in fact become a Master of Foxhounds. His fellow-artists jocosely observed that he was going to the dogs. His obituary in *The Times* of 7 January 1935, recorded:

There was no special sporting tradition in the Aldin family, so far as we know, but whether it was his early association with a scratch (and very mangy) pack kept by a butcher at Midhurst or the gift of a broken-down polo pony when he went to live in Chiswick, it is certain that from an early age his aspiration was to hunt. Knowing very little about it, he had the audacity to offer his services as a hunting correspondent to one of the better-known sporting papers, and, much to his astonishment, his offer was accepted. He actually hunted from Chiswick, after the manner of Jorrocks, with Metropolitan packs. That began it; and by the time that ill-health stopped his active career he had hunted his own pack of harriers, beagles, the South Berkshire Foxhounds, and, latterly, Mr Godfrey Heseltine's pack of Basset hounds, and had hunted the fox in upwards of thirty counties.

This passage shows how desperately anxious artists were not to be thought arty; even Phil May was obviously pleased to be called 'sporting'.

Aldin, born in 1870, was educated at Eastbourne College, and Solihull Grammar School. He studied anatomy at South Kensington, and animal painting under Frank W. Calderon. His first drawing was published in *The Graphic* in 1891, and he illustrated Kipling's Jungle Stories for the *Pall Mall Budget*, 1894–5. His first poster was for Colman's washing blue. Illustrated in *The Poster* as the frontispiece to the December, 1899 issue, it shows a French peasant, Millet-style, harrowing with two white horses and wearing a blue smock. To a man who could introduce two horses into an advertisement for a washday commodity, it was nothing to introduce four into a poster for

Phil May, poster for an exhibition of his own drawings at the Fine Art Society.

CECIL
ALPIN

COLMAN'S
BLUE

Bemrose & Sons, Lᵗᵈ Derby & London.

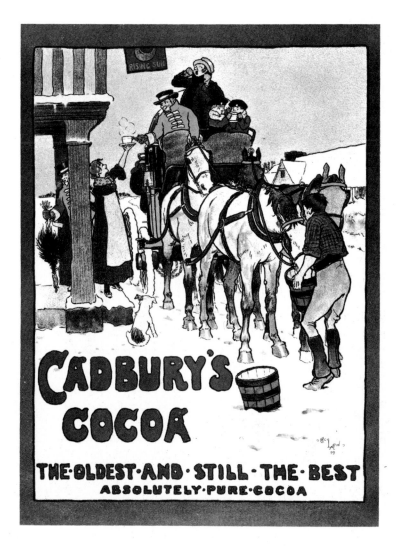

Cecil Aldin, poster for
Cadbury's Cocoa, 1899.

opposite Cecil Aldin, poster for
Colman's (washing) blue, 1899.

Cadbury's Cocoa, which was first illustrated in *The Poster* of February 1900. The inevitable dog in 'Your grandfathers drank Ellis Davies' Tea' has been mentioned; when Hassall caricatured Aldin for *The Poster* of December, 1899, he showed him clutching one dog, with another peering suspiciously from behind his right leg. On the wall is a childish drawing labelled 'A Dog', satirizing Aldin's plagiarism of Hassall's creation.

A poster by Lewis Baumer was illustrated in the first issue of *The Poster* (June, 1898): a design for *Cassell's Magazine*. By one of those phenomenally sustained careers, matched in this century by Erté, Van Dongen and Maurice Chevalier, he was still drawing cartoons for *Punch* in the 1960s. His best poster was for O. K. sauce: a girl in a cafe is delicately opening a bottle above the caption 'Saucy but quite O. K.'. The representationalism with which the bottle-label is drawn contrasts oddly with the impressionistic suggestion of the figure. In fact, this effectively

Cecil Aldin, poster for
Ellis Davies' tea, 1899.

opposite Caricature of Cecil Aldin by
John Hassall. In the background,
Hassall makes fun of Aldin's version
of the 'Hassall dog'.

draws attention to the product; although it was a persistent
complaint of posterists at this time that manufacturers who
commissioned posters ruined the design by insisting on a
minutely faithful presentation of their product.

Stewart Browne was originally trained as a designer for calico
printing in Glasgow. He then went to the Manchester School of
Art, where he took up figure drawing, and later studied at South
Kensington and Heatherley's. As with Hassall and Aldin, his
first published drawings appeared in *The Graphic*. The first firm
of printers he joined, he told the *Poster* interviewer in April,
1899, was Clement Smith. Browne was advanced enough as far
as throwing out Victorian grundyism was concerned: the wonder
is that the first picture to be published in *The Poster*, which he
contributed, was ever allowed to appear. But, though a relentless
professional, he never managed to rid himself of old-fashioned
concepts of design he learnt in his training. He belonged very

much to the cram-as-much-as-you-can-into-every-poster school, and the *Poster* interviewer also suggested that he belonged to the 'bloodstained melodramatic' style in his theatrical posters.

His namesake Tom Browne, whose posters are of a similar type (that for Raleigh Cycles shows a solar topee'd British officer wheeling away a harem beauty while the sultan looks on in fury) served a seven years' apprenticeship, mainly with Grovers of Nottingham. Then he began drawing for Cassell's. His posters fail for the most part because they are merely blown-up cartoons. One, showing a Scotsman being caught by a customs officer with a bottle of Roderick Dhu Highland Whisky in his bag, has what must be the longest and dreadfullest caption on any poster:

Customs House Officer: 'I thought you said you only had wearing apparel in the bag.'
MacNab: 'Hoots, mon, so I did. That's only my *night cap*, ye ken.'

Browne, another member of the London Sketch Club, is true to type. *The Poster* of October, 1899 reported:

Mr Browne had some great adventures in Spain and in the most savage districts, positively carried his life in his hands and a *revolver in a knapsack*.
He actually undertook a tandem ride from Paris to Gibraltar, plugging through hot weather, snow, and five days' continuous rain.
He is fond of athletics, rides a gee-gee, likes boxing, and keeps a stout pair of single sticks ready for interviewers ...
'I was in Paris during the recent troubles at the Grand Prix. There were four of us, we felt jolly and sang "John Brown's Knapsack" as we strolled along. Suddenly we were surrounded by fierce gendarmes and arrested.'

Among all these hearties, Walter Crane remained a defiant aesthete. But, like Tom Browne, he was able to achieve nothing more in his posters than an enlargement of his ordinary graphic style. *The Poster* of March, 1899, said Crane had chosen 'the rich riot of the Renaissance rather than the sombre and hard Gothic which Mr Morris seemed to prefer.' His posters for Hau champagne, for his own designs, for the Law Union and Crown Insurance Company and the Scottish Widows' Provident Institution, are admirable wall decoration, but the viewer has to disentangle the message, in each case, from an imbroglio of lines and vines and arabesques.

Harry Furniss was the prolific *Punch* cartoonist who invented Gladstone's huge collars. He, too, found difficulty in changing his style when he turned to poster work – but his natural cartoon manner was so bold and flamboyant that it translated easily on to the hoardings. At times his interpretation was not felicitous: it is hard to imagine anyone attracted into drinking Bovril by

Walter Crane, poster for an exhibition of his own designs at the Fine Art Society.

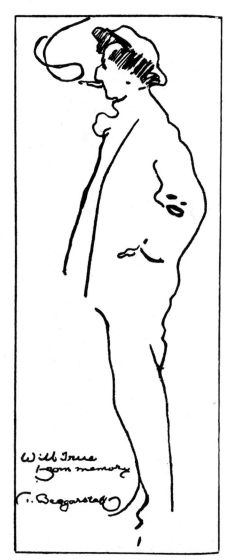

James Pryde, caricature of Will True from memory, signed 'J. Beggarstaff': published in *The Poster* of July, 1898.

opposite 'M. Yendis' (Sidney Ransom), cover design for the first issue of *The Poster*, June, 1898. The poppy motif, with its suggestion of opium and 'sin', is a recurring one in Art Nouveau, and is also seen in one of Hassall's Little Red Riding Hood posters. Note, too, the Mucha-style hair patterns.

the picture of a feathered African chief leering insanely into a bottle of it. But Furniss also designed one of the most successful of all posters, that for Pears Soap which showed a filthy old tramp with the caption 'Ten years ago, I used your soap: since then, I have used no other.'

Albert Morrow studied at South Kensington, where he won an exhibition. While there, his work attracted the attention of Comyns Carr, editor of *The English Illustrated Magazine*, who commissioned him to illustrate a series on English industries. His first poster, published by Clement Smith, was a blood-and-thunder design for 'The Stranglers of Paris; or, the Grip of Iron'. Morrow told the *Poster* interviewer (March, 1899) that Clement Smith had produced several posters by Phil May before May went to Australia. 'Some of them, I think, were done to advertise "The Private Secretary". As you may imagine these would fetch high prices if any copies of them could be traced.'

'Then you are an admirer of Phil May, Mr Morrow?'
'Rather! Who isn't an admirer of Phil May nowadays?'

Morrow's best-known posters were for the paper *Illustrated Bits*, with a dancing girl swirling chiffon in the Loïe Fuller manner; and for the play *The New Woman* by Sidney Grundy – a monocled Miss surrounded by the débris of study and cigarette ends. He told *The Poster*:

I think that the lettering should form an essential part of the design. When I leave it to the printers the result is generally horrible. I may say, while we are talking of poster making, that I consider the mechanical enlargement of a design altogether wrong. Formerly, I used to paint my posters full size in distemper, but I have been compelled to abandon this system, although I am more convinced than ever that it is the only proper one.

Will True, born in 1866, came strongly under Beggarstaff influence. (There is a caricature of him by Pryde, signed 'J. Beggarstaff'). But his first allegiance was to Chéret. He began life as a post-office clerk in Glasgow, tapping out telegraph codes. His artistic career began on the *Glasgow Evening News*, the first illustrated daily in Britain, under the editorship of J. M. Smith. The styles of his posters, as one might expect from his mixed influences, vary greatly; the *Poster* interviewer who visited his 'Oriental' studio in July, 1898, called him 'the most versatile posterist of the day'.

'Mosnar Yendis' was the topsy-turvy pseudonym of Sidney Ransom, perhaps the best English posterist after the Beggarstaffs. Interviewed by *The Poster* in September, 1899, he acknowledged an influence not mentioned by the other posterists.

I asked who, in his opinion, was entitled to be considered the 'Poster King' – the title having been conferred on several – to which he replied:

'Decidedly, Mucha, the Hungarian, and I think his work holds first place in the affections of most posterists. His designs, colour and drawing are beyond criticism, but the results would be very different if his beautiful designs were printed in England. I can imagine the feelings of Mucha if he suffered from English printers. O. de Rycker, of Brussels, who prints Privat-Livemont's work, and Champenois, of Paris, are lithographic printers *par excellence.*'

His poster for the 'Szalay' home trainer is a characteristic blend of humour, prominent lettering, and a heavily stylized design. Yendis also designed the cover of the first issue of *The Poster*; the Art Nouveau pattern of poppyheads, orange hair, and white arms, with the grim mysterious figure (Sleep? Death?) in the background, is one of the best they ever used. Hassall's interpretation of a similar theme in December, 1898 makes an amusing contrast: the commercial appeal of Hassall's work (as a poster for a pantomime) is obvious, yet how much more subtle is Yendis's study in pale ochre, mandragora green, misty blues and black.

Yendis was despondent about the future of the poster:

Wall advertising is at present far from ideal, and the neck and neck race between the correct poster and the unspeakable interloper will perhaps end in a foul, to the ultimate extermination of both. Advertisers have had ample time to discover the superiority of the artistic poster. They have had their atrocities swamped by simple designs; they have been talked to seriously, and they have been laughed at, but it makes no difference ... Take a large hoarding; for every good poster you will find twenty horrors. The billsticker arranges them all with a sublime indifference to harmony and balance – ergo, utter chaos!

But at this time, the 'artistic poster' was still a very new art form and advertising medium. Not until the 1920s would most manufacturers assimilate the lessons that Yendis and his friends had tried to teach them: that simplicity sells; that the caption need not be a *novella*; that art is no deterrent.

opposite 'M. Yendis', poster for the Szalay home trainer.

Design by Will True from *The Poster*, June, 1898.

America to 1914

In the Tudor period, many of the English public schools of today had not been founded. Those that had, were 'free schools', that is, grammar schools like the rest; and Shakespeare attended a grammar school. But by the eighteenth century, Eton had become the leading school in the country, a nursery for the great. It educated Gray, Horace Walpole, Fox and Shelley. With Dr Arnold's Rugby, in the nineteenth century, the public school system and the public school manner and the old boy network, the power of the old school tie, were established. It is really only in the last twenty-five years that Britain has seen that power eroded by the so-called 'classless society', and seen the system exposed in films like Lindsay Anderson's *If* and threatened with elimination by state control.

In the Victorian period, even an Etonian like Gladstone could still be a target (though hardly a victim) of snobbery because his grandfather and father were tainted by trade: Algernon West wrote of him that he was looked down on by 'the ruling classes' because 'he was not bred in their kennel'. The *carrière ouverte au talent* was a French theory, not an English practice. So it is extraordinary to find that three men who were exact contemporaries at Brighton Grammar School in the late 1880s all became eminent: Aubrey Beardsley; Charles Cochran (later Sir Charles), the impresario who staged Noël Coward's revues and brought Mistinguett, Sarah Bernhardt and Chaliapin to England; and George Frederick Scotson-Clark, a posterist who became art editor of *The Century* magazine in America and was also described as 'a second Sainte-Beuve' from his several books on cookery. The origins of the modern American poster owe much to these three English contemporaries. Beardsley's drawings were probably the most powerful influence on American poster art, certainly on the art of their greatest posterist, Will Bradley. Other American posterists, such as Claude Fayette Bragdon, were less successful in assimilating the influence of Beardsley's designs.

Cochran and Scotson-Clark were artistic missionaries who went to America: Scotson-Clark designed posters there which introduced Americans to the new French-influenced style; while Cochran was the first to chronicle the early development of the American pictorial poster in *The Poster* magazine.

Let us begin with Cochran, the only one of the three who wrote books of memoirs. He was admitted to Brighton Grammar School after being expelled from Eastbourne College. In *Secrets of a Showman* (1925) he wrote:

On my first day at dinner I sat next to a delicate-looking boy, thin, red-haired, and with a slight stoop. He was a particularly quick talker, used his hands to gesticulate, and altogether had an un-English air

Will H. Bradley: poster for *The Chap-Book*, 1894. The influence of Beardsley is strong in this swirling composition, known as 'The Twins'.

129

Claude Fayette Bragdon, 'A Wilde
Night', like most of his designs a
rather ham-fisted pastiche of Beardsley.

about him. I did right to note him well, for he was Aubrey Beardsley, the odd, fantastic, brilliant artist who, in the all too short time that he lived, earned a fame that spread through two hemispheres. When we talked, we found that both of us had a feeling for the stage. Even in those days Beardsley preferred Congreve and Wycherley to the ordinary books of boyhood. Before long, Beardsley and I were allowed to share a private study. We were under a master, Mr A.W. King, who also was very fond of theatrical entertainment, and it was largely through him that almost every week some performance was given. Beardsley and I became quite prominent. We played *Ici on Parle Français*; Beardsley was the Frenchman and I took Toole's old part. We also did *The Spitalfields Weaver* and I remember, too, reciting 'Ostler Joe' and Beardsley gave a most impressive rendering of 'Eugene Aram'. There was one special occasion when the school gave a Christmas performance of the *Pied Piper* at the Dome.

Cochran kept up his friendship with Beardsley until the latter's death in 1898, and Beardsley gave him two early drawings, one of Ellen Terry and one of Zola. Cochran also later contributed an article to *The Poster* magazine on Beardsley's schoolboy drawings. These drawings, illustrations to the programme of the *Pied Piper*, have not been taken into account by the various recent commentators on Beardsley, although they are fascinating evidence of the rapidity of his artistic development: for these early sketches are less accomplished than, for example, Max Beerbohm's schoolboy cartoons of his music teacher and headmaster at Charterhouse (sold at Sotheby's on 11 March 1968), while, by 1893, Beardsley was an acclaimed master. In *Secrets of a Showman*, Cochran describes how the article was written:

> I remember sitting up one night to write an article on Aubrey Beardsley's schooldays, which I sold the next morning to Sidney Ransom, who was running a paper called *The Poster*. I had no fire in the studio, it was bitterly cold, and I was hungry. The article was actually written for my breakfast! Ransom was very generous; I do not remember the exact sum he gave me, but it was something quite handsome for so small a publication.

In the same book, Cochran describes his other Brighton contemporary, Scotson-Clark: 'He was a strange, impressive youth. He had his own ideas about music and literature and life generally; he was the son of the composer of the "*Marché aux Flambeaux*". He could also draw, and indeed ultimately became art editor of the *Century Magazine*.' In another book, *Cock-a-doodle-do*, Cochran tells how he, Beardsley and Scotson-Clark all took part in a school performance of *Box and Cox*: Scotson-Clark was Mrs Bouncer, Cochran was Box, and Beardsley, Cox.

In 1891, Cochran said to Scotson-Clark: 'Let's go to America;

G. F. Scotson-Clark, 'Henry Irving',
1900.

opposite Advertisement by Bird for a
poster exhibition in 1895, the height of
the 'poster craze' in America.

I will earn my living on the stage; you will become a painter.'
From Boulogne they went steerage by a Holland-America liner,
the *Werkendam.* They would not stay in their sleeping quarters
because of 'the filthy habits of our fellow-travellers – largely
Lithuanians and Poles'. Soon after their arrival in New York,
they tried for a job as 'supers' in the New York Yacht Club
scene of *An American Citizen*, but the producer, Joseph Brooke
(who later brought *Ben Hur* over to Drury Lane), rejected the
eighteen-year-old Cochran as too juvenile-looking. Scotson-
Clark, who looked older, was engaged at one dollar a performance, and shared what he earned with Cochran. Scotson-
Clark had brought to America a top hat and a black Inverness
cape – 'He looked quite an impressive figure. He posed as my
manager, said that I was a talented young singer of comic songs,
and tried to get me engagements. But it was heart-breaking
work.' At last Cochran was engaged to sing at Huber's (opposite
Tammany Hall), a dime museum where freaks were exhibited:
the dog-faced boy, Jonathan Bass; the ossified man, the skeleton
dude, the fat lady, the tattooed man, and the man who wrote
with his toes. On one floor a variety performance was given, for
which ten cents were charged. Cochran sang there at thirty
dollars a week, and had some success with the songs he had so
recently been trolling out at cosy Brighton smoking-concerts.

James Cleugh in *Charles B. Cochran, Lord Bountiful*, gives a
racy portrait of New York as it was when Cochran and Scotson-
Clark arrived:

New York in the 'nineties was a sprawling, untidy but eminently
picturesque city: very different from its neat, economically planned
and scyscraping successor of today. There were not many high buildings, though more than in any European town. Mule-drawn tramcars
rattled along briskly between rows of smallish and rather dirty-looking
shops. Many of the houses in the residential quarters were still rickety
wooden structures bearing the impermanent aspect associated with
early colonial settlements. Fruit-stalls stood at every corner, piled with
huge green melons and little black grapes. Pig-tailed Chinamen and
coal-black negroes, together with every type of mixture between these
and the European races, abounded in the crowded streets. Com-
paratively few women were to be seen. Half the male population, if
white, went about 'heeled' with conspicuous six-shooters and wore
tremendous hats. Spidery-looking four-wheeled 'buggies' and two-
wheeled 'sulkies', drawn by leggy thoroughbreds, shot about like
lightning through and round irregular squares of incongruously
countrified appearance. Finally, there was the Bowery, which young
Mr Cochran was to come to know very well indeed in the next few
years. Few Englishmen found their way there. The life of the in-
habitants of this district – named from the Dutch word for a peasant –
was almost as lawless as in the Wild West.

POSTER
EXHIBIT

MECHAN-
ICS FAIR
THE 19TH EX-
HIBITION

A·D·1895

ENGRAVED BY THE SUFFOLK ENGRAVING CO BOSTON.

BIRD

BANK OF ENGLAND
Robbed of a Million
by the aid of
NEW YORK POLICE

A Remarkable Story of
Corruption That Can
Hardly Listen.

DO DEAD COME BACK?

Spiritualism in a New Light
by the Psychical Society

NAPOLEON IN NEW YORK

HEILIG IN PARIS

THE NEW YORK RECORDER

SUNDAY

Next
Sunday's
Recorder
Will
Be
The
Brightest,
Newsiest,
Best
And
Most
Interesting
Newspaper
Published
In
America.

ORDER FROM
Your Newsdealer in Advance.

JAN? 6.
1895.

G. F. Scotson-Clark, poster for the
New York Recorder, 1895.

The two men arrived in New York in 1891. In Chicago, in 1890, Will Bradley had already designed his superb poster for Tom Hall's *When Hearts are Trumps*. But New York was an artistic desert; the only oasis was Hoffman House in Madison Square, which Phil May called 'the National Gallery of America' – a bar hung with pictures, patronized by 'Western' millionaires in wonderful sombreros, their tie-pins made from rough nuggets of gold. In an article on 'Theatrical Posters in America' which he contributed to *The Poster* of July, 1898, Cochran wrote:

Seven years ago, when I first visited America, I was struck with the horrors that looked down upon one from the hoardings. The huge theatrical posters, although beautifully printed, were entirely lacking in taste as regards design and colour. The figures were tailors' dummies without life or movement, and the backgrounds were the old stereotyped German photographic reproductions of scenes from the play advertised. Things in the States are very different now, and with the exception of a few purveyors of cheap melodrama, the American impresario strives his utmost to secure original and tasteful designs from first-rate artists.

What had produced the change? Partly the Mucha posters that Sarah Bernhardt brought with her on her American tour; though the actress who had assured Bastien-Lepage, when he was painting her portrait, that 'if I sit still, I will make *you* famous', was not delighted to see a cruel parody of her cadaverous features staring down from a poster which proclaimed 'Carter's River Bitters will Make You Eat'. Partly the early posters for newspapers by Scotson-Clark, which, although crude in drawing, showed a perfect understanding of how the medium should be exploited. His poster for the *New York Recorder* (according to *The Poster* of January 1899) was the first illustrated poster ever designed to advertise an American daily newspaper. But it was in 1894 that the poster craze really took hold of New York, when Eugene Tompkins heralded a revival of the play *The Black Crook* with a number of Chéret posters. The collecting fever spread, and in January 1896 it was estimated that there were more than 6,000 poster collections in the United States. Ambrose Bierce, author of *The Devil's Dictionary*, satirized the cult in the *New York Journal*, in particular its high priest, Percival Pollard, who was to write the introduction to Edward Penfield's *Book of the Poster* (1898):

Mr Percival Pollard is our best American authority on posters and poster lore. With Mr Pollard the poster is not a fad, but a cult. He adores it with the same enthusiasm and self-consecration that inspires the Hindu man-and-brother when contemplating the ligneous virtues and hand-painted pulchritude of the Idol of Hope and Slaughter. I don't care to affirm an equality between these two objects of worship; the Idol is the prettier, but the poster is incomparably superior in that it lends itself to the art of the collector and thereby invites an affection that is not necessarily an element of worship. Whatever one can collect one can learn to love with a warm and tender regard which deity, even of one's own facture, does not always inspire. I once knew a collector of champagne corks, each of which he duly labelled with the date of its popping and such other details of its history as he knew or could ascertain. He had a bushel, and I am persuaded that his relations with each unit of the lot had something of the charm and tenderness of an intrigue. I dare say that in the secret soul of him my friend Pollard cherishes for the green blondes and yellow brunettes of his collection a sentiment that ought to land him in the divorce court. These earthly emotions he will keep to himself, and being a capital writer will doubtless make many a convert to his funny faith, but as for me, I feel as yet no call to go forward to the anxious seat, but with a wicked and stiff-necked perversity purpose continuing in my state of sin, regarding the poster with contumelious irreverence.

Before discussing the native American posterists, we should perhaps turn back briefly to Scotson-Clark. What Cochran has to tell us about him ends abruptly when the two part company; and it is a measure of the show-biz mogul's egocentricity that he shows no further interest in the fortunes of the friend who had shared his small wage with him when he had none. No interest, at any rate, is recorded in his huge rambling autobiographies; though a passage about Scotson-Clark in Cochran's *Poster* article of June 1898 suggests that loyalty at least had survived in a friendship which had been subjected to the strain of hard times. All the same, the coolness of the objectivity Cochran applies is suspicious:

About a year after the appearance of Mr Tompkins' Chéret posters, New York found itself staring at a curious looking yellow girl who proclaimed herself to be 'The Twentieth Century Girl'. Among her commonplace surroundings on the hoardings this young lady was most conspicuous. Little knots of people gathered in the streets to stare at her, and the enterprising Yankee pressman found much food for paragraphs at her expense. Her origin was discussed, and, as signed posters were then an unknown quantity in America, it was some time before the name of Scotson-Clark was found modestly prescribed in a corner. Now came a rush on Scotson-Clark. His work, although varying in quality, was seldom, if ever, without some phase of originality, and if it was not always all that could be desired from an artistic point of view, it was sure to possess some striking feature which made it effective from the advertiser's standpoint. His best posters have been two American twenty-four sheet [i.e. forty-eight sheet according to the English standard] 'stands' for 'The French Maid' and 'Little Christopher Columbus'.

opposite G. F. Scotson-Clark, poster for the literary journal *The Bookman*.

THE BOOKMAN

A LITERARY JOURNAL

APRIL
NUMBER
NOW READY

DODD, MEAD AND COMPANY. 5th AVE. & 21st STREET, NEW YORK

At first, Scotson-Clark had made a living in New York as a stage designer, of scenery and accessories: he designed the costumes for productions of *The Girl from Paris* (an American version of *The Gay Parisienne*), *The French Maid*, and *Excelsior Junior*. His first poster was that for the *New York Recorder*. In 1895 he designed an advertisement for the American *Bookman*, showing an old mumpsimus in long, black, Beardsleyesque robes running his finger across an illuminated book. He produced several posters for the *New York World*, and others to advertise George Macdonald's novel *Lilith*, and *The Gallic Girl*, an American translation of a volume by the French writer 'Gyp'. For the *New York Ledger*, he designed three placards, and three more for *Outing*. In 1897 he returned to England, where he designed a double crown bill for *Oh, Susannah!* and effective placards for Penley's *Little Ray of Sunshine* and *Tommy Dodd*, for *The Lady Slavey* and *Bilbury of Tilbury*. The influence of Pryde on his work is very evident in his poster of Irving and in the cover he designed for his own book on the music-halls. In an interview full of sub-Beardsley epigrams and sub-Beerbohm conceit, published first in *Unwin's Chap Book* and later in *The Poster* of January, 1900, he said:

I am the boy wonder. I lisped in outlines, for the outlines came. I did not learn to draw, I drew. I was already a boy wonder at seven, and of course I've grown more of a boy wonder ever since. The sole object of many years of struggle and adventures was to increase my youthful precocity. That is why, being at school when youth was at its dawn, I had Aubrey Beardsley for companion, and resolved with him to achieve a name in fame and art ... I opened a studio in New York, and began to design. A new idea came to realization. The picture poster for the daily newspaper. I – *moi qui vous parle* – I designed the first picture poster ever issued for a daily paper. It advertised the *New York Recorder*. From the *New York Recorder* I passed to *The World*. I worked for *The World* for a year, and then in turn left that for the *Journal*. There were difficulties. The printers of the lithographic houses struck against me because I was not a member of their Union. Would I join? Of course not. I was an artist, not an artisan. I won. Of course I won. But I thought it better to turn home again. It took seven years of America to make me as young as I am.

As with Byron or d'Annunzio, one suspects that Scotson-Clark's talent was more for being romantic than for dedicating himself to his art. The last we hear of him before he finally decided that his genius lay rather in *crêpes suzettes* and *coquilles St-Jacques* than in posters and placards, is an article he contributed to *The Poster* of November, 1900, entitled 'The Black Spot in America'. This was a perceptive study of Beardsley's influence on the American poster. As Scotson-Clark was writing fewer than ten

W.S. Penley

PRINCE OF WALES THEATRE,
SIX NIGHTS
MONDAY, AUG. 20.

A LITTLE RAY OF SUNSHINE

BY
MARK AMBIENT
&
WILTON HERIOT

Scotson Clark

WEINERS LTD WYBERT ST LONDON. N.W.

Will Bradley, a tender and imaginative
design for *The Inland Printer*, 1894.

THE·INLAND·PRINTER

Will Bradley could command a more powerful style. This design for *The Inland Printer*, of wind-bent trees reflected in a lagoon, is convincing evidence that Bradley was much more than an imitator of Beardsley.

years after the works he describes and illustrates were produced, the article has more the status of an historical document than of an academic appraisal:

Until the winter of 1894, the artistic poster was practically unknown in the United States. The only things of the kind, and they were very excellent and very original, were the *Harper's Magazine* window bills by Edward Penfield. But during the latter part of 1893, and the early half of 1894, the name and work of Aubrey Beardsley had become known, and popular as was his success amongst a large class in England, his fame was tenfold in America. Every twopenny-halfpenny town had its 'Beardsley Artist', and the large cities simply teemed with them. Some borrowed his ideas and adapted them to their own uses; others imitated, till one asked oneself: 'Is this done by the English or American B?'

The 'American B' was Will H. Bradley, whom Scotson-Clark put first among the School of Beardsley:

Advertisers now began to see that, given an effective design, by using a few flat colours, a better result and a cheaper advertisement could be obtained. Consequently the Beardsley artist set to work. In this line Bradley was certainly first favourite, and his output was enormous. As far as I know, he only did one large poster, an American twenty-four-sheet Stand [twenty-eight English Double Crowns] for Frohman's production of *The Masqueraders*. But he did a one-sheet for *Hood's Sarsaparilla*, which was not at all bad from an advertising point of view. Then he did several for the Chicago *Chap Book*, and also for the *Inland Printer*. The latter were for covers, but were also, I believe, used for posters. For mercantile houses he did several, also for his own publication, *Bradley, his Book*. Clever though he undoubtedly is, I do not think he would ever have adopted the class of work in which he has become known had not Beardsley set the example. Until the latter had introduced it, people did not understand the use of the 'black blot' as an element in composition. Although it had been used years before in England in the famous 'Woman in White', by Fred Walker, no one seemed to realize that the solid black mass could be utilized in a decorative way.

We are lucky that Will Bradley wrote a memoir of his life, published by the New York Typophiles as *Will Bradley: His Chap Book* in 1955. He tells his story with great vivacity, revealing a modest and engaging personality reminiscent of that of another artist autobiographer, E. H. Shepard, the English book illustrator. Like John Hassall, Bradley was born in 1868. His father was a cartoonist on the *Daily Item*, the newspaper of Lynn, Massachusetts. Lynn was a shoe town, with a strongly religious population – Universalists and Unitarians. Women worked at home, binding the uppers and tongues of high-laced shoes. Young Bradley had a little express wagon in which he

Caricature of Bradley, in a parody of Beardsley's style, by Will True.

carried finished work back to the factories, returning with a supply of unfinished. For each trip he received five cents. With his savings, he bought a printing press, the kind you put on a table and slammed with the palm of your hand. It was the sort of machine used in business offices to stamp date lines. In 1874 his father brought him home a box of 'pi', and when Bradley had found a few letters of the same font he filed them to fit the type slot in the press.

His father was ill, as a result of the Civil War. The family moved to the section called Swampscott, too far away for Bradley to attend the school to which his class had gone. His mother went out every day to dress-making. Most of the time, Bradley stayed at home with his father. When Bradley Senior died in 1877, Bradley and his mother moved to Ishpeming, a mining town in northern Michigan, where his mother had a sister whose husband was paymaster at the Lake Superior Iron Mine. Every night Bradley knelt down and prayed God to tell his uncle to bring him a printing press like those shown in *The Youth's Companion*. His uncle brought him an Ingersoll dollar watch.

In 1880, Bradley took his first job, at three dollars a week, as a printer's devil with the *Iron Agitator* (later *Iron Ore*). The owner and editor was George A. Newett, who was later sued for libel by Theodore Roosevelt. (The trial took place in Marquette, Michigan, and Roosevelt was awarded six cents.) Bradley was put to work washing a Gordon press, then had his first lesson in 'feeding'. By the age of twelve, he was setting type, dealing with advertising display, and making up the paper. His wages were increased to six dollars a week. When the motor power failed, as it often did, he would go on to the street and employ off-shift miners to work the press by a crank attached to the flywheel. He worked in the print shop, which was over a saloon, from seven a.m. until six p.m.

Across the street was the *Peninsula Record*, a four-page tabloid which was printed one page at a time on a large Gordon press. The owner and editor, John D. West, offered Bradley eight dollars a week. With the extra two dollars, he was able to start saving. When the *Iron Ore* moved into a new store building, Newett offered him ten dollars a week and the recognized post of job printer. At fourteen, this was increased to twelve dollars. At fifteen, he was foreman, and receiving fifteen dollars – a man's wages in 1883.

The West was still Wild. One of Bradley's anecdotes of his early days sounds like the opening of a 'B' movie:

This is the early Eighties. Small towns such as Ishpeming are 'easy

Will Bradley, poster for Victor Bicycles: the eye is forced to separate the message from a tangle of foliage.

pickings' for travelling fakers. Their advance is always heralded by the exchanges. They clean up at the expense of local merchants. All editors warn them to keep away. *Iron Ore* print shop is on the ground floor. The editor's sanctum is at the front. His desk is at the big window. It is nearly nine o'clock on a Friday night – 'makeup' time. Mr Newett has written his last sheets of copy and is reading proof. At the corner of Main and Division, diagonally across from the office, a faker is selling soap. In one wrapper he pretends to place a five-dollar bill – a version of the 'old army game'. He is standing in a market wagon and has a companion who strums a guitar and sings. Attached to an upright and above his head is a kerosene flare. Mr Newett walks leisurely to where there are several guns and fishing rods in a corner. He is an inveterate sportsman in a land where game, deer and fish, is plentiful. Selecting a rifle he walks to the door and casually puts a bullet through the kerosene tank, then returns to his proof reading.

Bradley and a compositor had charge of the town's bill-posting. He was now sixteen, almost seventeen. One day he was designing a masquerade poster for the roller rink, when he was talent-spotted by Frank Bromley, a landscape painter from Chicago. He told Bradley to come and see him there. Bradley set out for Chicago with eighty dollars (four twenty-dollar gold pieces) he had saved. Bromley had a studio near the McVickar Theater on Madison Street. 'It was the typical *atelier* of the Victorian 'eighties – oriental drapes, screens and pottery. Jules Guerin, then an art student and later a contributor to *The Century*, *Harper's* and *Scribner's* was cleaning up for the day.' Bromley obtained Bradley a job at Rand McNally in Monroe Street, as an apprentice in the designing department. Bromley also found him a room at the house of a friend, an art dealer at Vincennes Avenue and 59th Street. At this stage, Bradley imagined that designers did their own engraving. He himself was learning to engrave tints on woodblocks. But after a few weeks it occurred to him that as the wood-engravers never seemed to do any designing, perhaps designers never did any engraving. So, as he was down to his last gold piece, he returned to the printing shop in northern Michigan. But in 1887 he came back to Chicago to join Knight and Leonard, the city's leading fine printers, as a fully-fledged designer at twenty-one dollars and then twenty-four dollars a week. (Mr Leonard was the father of Lilian Russell, the actress, who once visited the office, to Bradley's delight.) There Bradley printed the first half-tone engravings in Chicago. There were no art magazines to inspire designers; so Bradley, like others, kept a scrap-book made up of booklet covers, cards, and other forms of advertising. The J. M. Jeffery Company, show printers, were turning out 'some swell posters'

Will Bradley, peacock feather design.

opposite Will Bradley, poster for Narcoti-cure, an early antidote to the 'tobacco habit'.

designed by Will Crane and printed from wood blocks. Frank Getty was designing labels for the Chicago office of the Crump Label Company, 'a glorious departure from the conventional truck of the label lithographers'. Bradley also admired the coloured paperback covers of Joe Lyendecker (another posterist), the railroad posters of Bridwell for Matthews Northrup in Buffalo, and the magazine illustrations of Abbey, Parsons, Frost, Pennell and Charles Graham in *Harper's Weekly*.

He now took a studio in the Caxton Building on Dearborn Street, and began freelance work, mainly for Kasten of the McClurg stationery department. He bought a Golding press, a type-stand, a small stone and a few cases of Caslon and an English text, on hire purchase. He was 'itching to play a little with printing'.

Bradley gives us a vivid impression of Chicago in the 1890s:

Chicago a phoenix city risen from the ashes of its great fire; downtown business buildings two, three and four stories high, more of former than latter, few a little higher, elevators a rare luxury; across the river many one-story stores and shops with signs in large lettering, pioneer-style, on their false fronts; streets paved with granite blocks echo to the rumble of iron-tired wheels and the clank of iron-shod hoofs; a continuous singing of steel car-cables on State Street and Wabash Avenue; horse-drawn cross-town cars thickly carpeted with straw in winter; outlying residential streets paved with cedar blocks; avenues boasting asphalt. Bonneted women with wasp waists, leg o'mutton sleeves, bustles, their lifted, otherwise dust-collecting, skirts revealing high-buttoned shoes and gaily-striped stockings; men in brown derbies, short jackets, high-buttoned waist-coats, tight trousers without cuffs and, when pressed, without pleats; shirts with Piccadilly collars and double-ended cuffs of detachable variety (story told of how a famous author's hero, scion of an old house, when travelling by train, saw a beautiful young lady, undoubtedly of aristocratic birth, possibly royal, and wanting to meet her, love at first sight, object matrimony, first retires, with true blue-blood gentility, to washroom and reverses cuffs. Romance, incident ruthlessly deleted by publisher, proves a best-seller.) Black walnut furniture upholstered in haircloth, pride of many a Victorian parlour, is gradually being replaced by golden oak and ash; painters' studios, especially portrait variety, are hung with oriental rugs and littered with oriental screens and pottery. High bicycles, the Columbia with its little wheel behind and the Star with the little wheel in front, soon to disappear, are still popular. Low wheels, called 'safeties', are beginning to appear, occasionally ridden by women wearing bloomers. Pneumatic tires unknown. Recognized now as a period of over ornamentation and bad taste, the Nineties were nevertheless years of leisurely contracts, kindly advice and an appreciative pat on the back by an employer, and certainly a friendly bohemianism seldom known in the rush and drive of today.

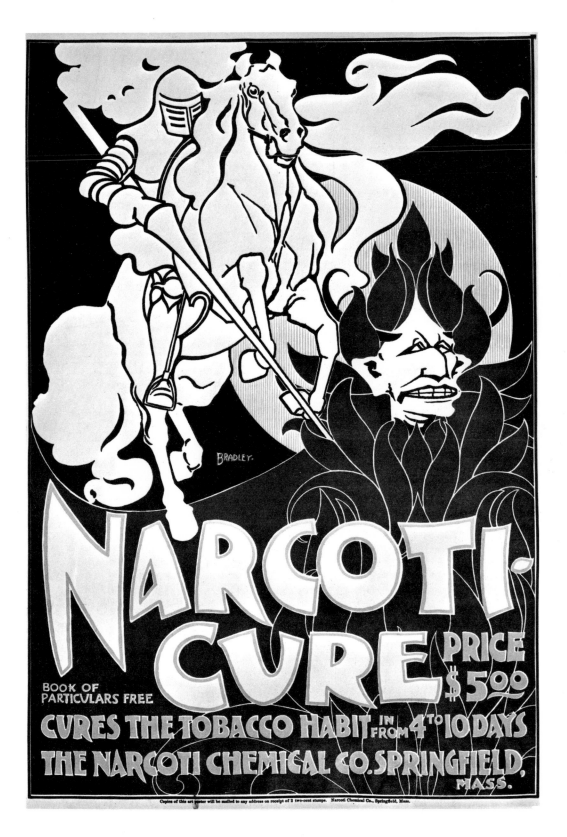

WHEN HEARTS ARE TRUMPS ♥ BY TOM HALL

Will Bradley's first poster, for Tom Hall's *When Hearts are Trumps*, 1890.

Eugene Field had just returned from a holiday in Europe, and in his column, 'Sharps and Flats', Chicago was reading the first printing of *Wynken, Blynken and Nod*. Way and Williams, publishers, had an office on the floor below Bradley's studio. Irving Way, who 'would barter his last shirt for a first edition, his last pair of shoes for a volume from the Kelmscott Press of William Morris', was a frequent and stimulating visitor. In 1890, Bradley got his first book assignment: Stone and Kimball commissioned a cover, title page, page decorations and poster for *When Hearts are Trumps* by Tom Hall. This recognition was followed by a meeting with Harriet Monroe and a Way and Williams commission for a cover and decorations for the *Columbian Ode*.

1893 was the year of the Chicago World's Fair, which gave Americans the chance to see what was happening in both European and Oriental art. Bradley had an exhibit that entitled him to a free pass. Buffalo Bill was appearing in a Wild West show. An edition of the humorous magazine *Puck* was being printed in one of the exhibition buildings. Shortly after the exhibition, Bradley began his series of brilliant covers for *The Inland Printer*, edited by McQuilkin and printed by Henry O. Shephard. They were the first magazine covers ever to be changed monthly. One of the covers, of a nymph in a pool, was later reproduced in *The Studio*, London. Another, a Christmas cover, included a panel of lettering that four American foundries and one German foundry began to cut as a type. Later the American Type Founders Company, paying for permission, named the face 'Bradley'.

In 1894, as we have seen, the poster craze swept America. Bradley's poster for *The Masqueraders* by Henry Arthur Jones, for the Empire Theatre, New York, was probably the first signed theatrical poster produced by any American lithographer. In this year, too, Bradley visited New York, where he saw show-bills set in Caslon type: they influenced all his later typographical work.

Now married, he moved to Geneva, Illinois, to a studio overlooking the Fox River. The commissions came pouring in, including covers for *Harper's Weekly*, *Harper's Bazaar* and *Harper's Young People*. Bradley was getting over-confident. As he later wrote, 'I was plucked before I was ripe'. He decided to set up his own printing business and start an art magazine. So in 1895 he settled in Springfield, Boston, opened the Wayside Press and published the first issue of his art journal, *Bradley: His Book*, in 1896. In the mid-nineties, compositors used random mixtures of the novelty faces which were all that the type foundries were casting. Bradley offered a startling alternative: a return to the Caslon faces to which printers had been restricted in the colonial

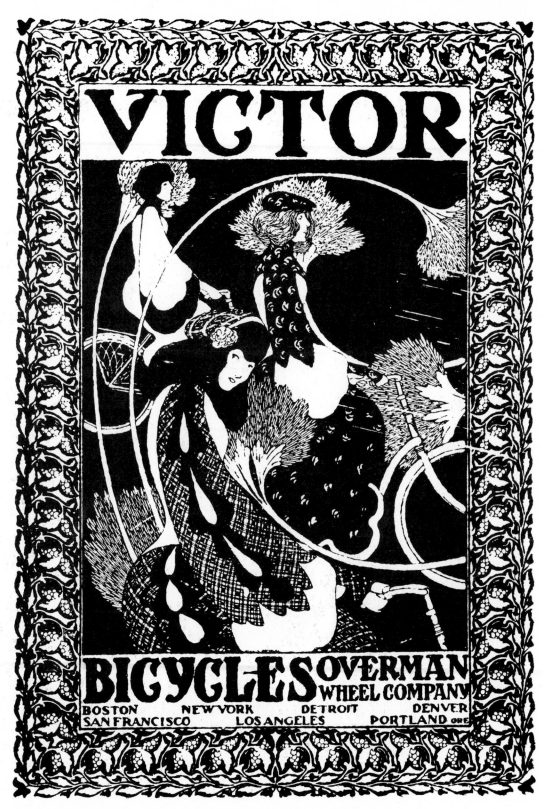

One design amusingly adapted for two posters: Bradley's advertisements for
Victor Bicycles (*above*) and Bar-lock typewriters (*opposite*).

BAR-LOCK

THE TYPEWRITER Co Lᵈ
12,14,16, QUEEN VICTORIA Sᵗ LONDON, E.C.

period, and which he had come to love in the Ishpeming print shop, and later by studying the Barton collection of Colonial New England books in the Boston Public Library. He contributed two or three cases of Wayside Press printing to the first exhibition of the Boston Society of Arts and Crafts held in Copley Hall in 1896. From the reviewers, he had flattering approval; but the printers laughed at him and said 'Bradley must be crazy if he thinks buyers of printing are going to fall for that old-fashioned Caslon type.' Less than a year later, the producers of Caslon could not keep pace with the demand. But Bradley had called his business the Wayside Press for a good reason. He had always intended to be, like his father, an artist. Printing was only on the wayside to achieving this; and he chose a dandelion leaf as his device, 'because the dandelion is a wayside growth'. In any case, he simply could not cope with the commercial printing business – vastly increased by a coalition with the Mittineague Paper Company in 1897 – and with editing and publishing *Bradley: His Book*. In 1898 his printing business was taken over by the University Press, Boston, and Bradley opened a design and art service in New York, with bicycle catalogues as his speciality. Again, he gives us a sharp vignette of the cultural scene:

And now we are in the Gay Nineties, the mid Gay Nineties, when a hair-cloth sofa adorns every parlour and over-decoration is running riot; when our intelligentsia are reading Anthony Hope's *Prisoner of Zenda*, Stanley Weyman's *Gentlemen of France* and George McCutcheon's *Graustark*; when William Morris is printing Chaucer, with illustrations by Burne-Jones, and Aubrey Beardsley is providing an ample excuse for the *Yellow Book*; when Le Gallienne's *Golden Girl* is brought over here by John Lane and established in a bookshop on Lower Fifth Avenue, and Bliss Carman is singing his songs of rare beauty.

This is the period in which Bradley's finest posters were designed: the beautiful bills for *The Chap-Book* with their elegant lettering of exemplary clarity; or the superb Art Nouveau advertisement for Victor Bicycles, later comically adapted into an equally good poster for the bar-lock typewriter; or the host of marvellously fanciful designs in black and white, which an authority on Beardsley who had never heard of Will H. Bradley would be bound to ascribe to the English master. The five *Chap-Book* posters are those for which he is best known. In an article on 'William H. Bradley and his Art' in *The Poster* of October, 1898, S. C. de Soissons christened them 'The Blue', 'The Pink', 'The Green', 'The Black' and 'The Red', from the dominant colour in each. 'In his most famous poster, which we call "The

opposite Will Bradley, poster for *The Chap-Book*, 1895. In this, the influence of William Morris is stronger than that of Beardsley.

The Chap-Book

Being A MISCELLANY of Curious and Interesting Songs, Ballads, Tales, Histories, &c.; adorned with a variety of pictures and very delightful to read: *newly composed* by MANY CELEBRATED WRITERS: To which are annex'd a LARGE COLLECTION of Notices of BOOKS

·WILL H BRADLEY·1895·

opposite Edward Penfield: this poster for Harper's shows Penfield's ability to convert a commonplace scene into a stylish design. The bled-off composition owes much to the Japanese print.

Bradley's poster for the Scribner volume, *The Modern Poster*. The legend in the bottom right-hand corner, 'Only one thousand copies printed of which this is No. 311', shows how publishers fed the American poster craze of 1895–6 with limited editions.

CHARLES SCRIBNER'S SONS
NEW YORK ❦ ❦ ❦ ❦ ❦ THE

WILL H BRADLEY 95

MODERN POSTER

ONLY ONE THOUSAND COPIES
PRINTED OF WHICH THIS IS NO 311

right Edward Penfield's self-portrait, a conventionally romantic face.

opposite Henry Mayor's caricature of Penfield, in *The Poster*, gives a rather different impression.

Blue", Bradley has displayed great skill by introducing the Japanese way of making pictures by a few coloured plain surfaces, such method being the source of the direction introduced into French art by Boutet de Monvel,* and having such a strong influence on the modern illustrations and artistic posters.'

From 1900, Bradley's career moves into high gear. He became art editor of several leading American journals, including *Collier's*, *Good Housekeeping* and *Pearson's*. He designed a new type face. While recovering from illness, he wrote a novel, *Castle Perilous*, later serialized in *Collier's* with illustrations by himself. From 1915 to 1917, he took over the art supervision of a motion picture series for William Randolph Hearst (Orson Welles's *Citizen Kane*), including *Patria*, starring Irene Castle. From 1918 to 1919 he was writing and directing films, and in 1920, became art and typography supervisor for Hearst magazines, newspapers, and motion pictures. He died in 1962, aged 94.

Because Bradley did not become a European apostate on the

* Louis-Maurice Boutet de Monvel (born Orléans 1851, died 1913). A pupil of five of the leading academic painters – Cabanel, Lefèbvre, Boulanger, Parrot and Carolus-Duran – he broke away from the academic tradition, under the influence of Japanese prints, and was one of the first to develop a 'silhouette' style.

This sketch by Edward Penfield, published in *Bradley: His Book*, 1896, shows how enthusiastically he succumbed to Japanese influence.

opposite Edward Penfield, a Gauguinesque poster for Richard Harding Davis's book *Three Gringos in Central America and Venezuela.*

Jamesian model, like Whistler, John Singer Sargent, or Mary Cassatt, American art historians have been tempted to characterize him as the all-American artist. William Dorwin Teague, for example, in his preface to Bradley's autobiography, calls him 'a native, corn-fed American', and says that America 'never had any more indigenous art than Bradley's'. As far as his typography is concerned, there is some truth in the latter suggestion, but what impresses one in a consideration of his art, his drawing and design and colour, is the astonishing sophistication and ability to assimilate foreign influence, in a man who could have remained a small-town hick with a print shop over a saloon. Mr Teague deplores Bradley's attempt to start the Wayside Press, and is glad that it failed: he sees it as a manifestation of the 'pious ambition' of the typographic designer 'to produce meticulous limited editions for equally limited collectors'.

Thank God it didn't work [he writes]. There was a lusty, democratic ambition in that slight body, and it thrilled him to speak to thousands, even millions, instead of just scores. The turbulent current of American commercial and industrial life appealed to him more than any exquisite backwater.

There is a lot of truth in this, too, but what it neglects to say is that in all those pious limited editions from the Kelmscott Press of Morris and the Vale Press of Ricketts, and again in the rarefied illustrations to the *Yellow Book*, Bradley found the springs of his artistic style. With Tiffany glass, it remains the most admirable expression of Art Nouveau in America.

When W. S. Rogers's book on posters was published in 1901, it was already possible to speak of Edward Penfield as a 'veteran in American poster art'. Yet he had been designing posters for Harper's for little more than a decade. When Bradley began poster work, Penfield was the only artist of his own country to whom he could look up, and he paid tribute to him in the first issue of *Bradley: His Book:*

He is like a tree that is well rooted, and strong in every branch. We have seen its leaves and flowers; they have sweetened the atmosphere of art; and now there is the ruddy fruit, and when we forget posters as a craze and value them as art, as a medium through which the artist speaks, then the fruit will have mellowed and ripened, and we shall realize better than now, the thought, care and patience necessary to bring it to that stage. Mr Penfield's work is wholly his own. It represents a thought; an expression; a mode of treatment which belongs to him alone; there is backbone to it. No matter what the pose, no matter what the idea, behind it all there is life, there is drawing, and good drawing. This alone marks him as a master; and in methods of reproduction, that difficult point to which so few give even a passing thought, he is a past master.

THREE GRINGOS IN CENTRAL
AMERICA AND VENEZUELA
BY RICHARD HARDING DAVIS
ILLUSTRATED
HARPER & BROTHERS · N·Y·

Maxfield Parrish, from a photograph reproduced in *The Book Buyer* of 1898.

opposite Edward Penfield, design for the March, 1894, issue of *Harper's*.

In the Harper's posters, and even more in the casual sketches Bradley reproduces with his article, we can see the paramount influence of the Japanese print on his work. Not only do the rabbits and hares look as if they have been lifted straight from a Hokusai *surimono* (the New Year's greeting card which gave Japanese artists the chance to translate their most insubstantial ideas into line, pictorial *haiku*); even the mouth and eyes of his women have a Japanese character. Almost certainly he was influenced by Lautrec too. His posters for Harper's and for Stearn's bicycles are the closest to Lautrec's in feeling, and they drew from *The Poster* magazine of August–September 1898 the kind of criticism that was continually levelled at Lautrec: 'It may be objected to Mr Penfield that his female faces are very plain and common-place and his women generally entirely devoid of "chic".' Young ladies should not be shown 'touzzled', as they put it, though for these critics the posters were thoroughly redeemed by the delightful animals, the mad March hare of the March issue, the Persian cats of the May one.

Maxfield Parrish has been overrated as a poster artist. Because of his undoubted excellence as a book illustrator, particularly of children's books on which critics are brought up and for which they form a sentimental attachment, no one has found it easy to admit that his posters are unsuccessful. Brian Howard and Peter Blake are among those who have greatly admired Parrish's book illustrations; and in reviewing Walt Reed's book *The Illustrator in America* in the *New York Times Book Review* of 19 February 1967, Nash K. Burger asked 'Was there a family without at least one Maxfield Parrish print?' But Parrish was a pointillist of the pen and a painter of never-never-lands. His posters for the Adlake camera and for the midsummer 1897 holiday number of the *Century* magazine are merely adaptations of that ubiquitous androgynous figure of his, crouched with hands clasped round knees in a leafy glade. It is close to the figure of the bubble-blower in what are probably his best set of book illustrations, those for Eugene Field's *Poems of Childhood*, that very strange and crypto-decadent book which no good Freudian would allow within seven leagues of a child.

He was the son of Stephen Parrish, the painter and etcher. After studying at Haverford College, he spent three years at the Pennsylvania Academy of Fine Arts, and then worked under Howard Pyle at the Drexel Institute: Pyle's illustrative work was obviously the cardinal influence on his work, both in its virtues and its faults. In 1898, Scribner's magazine, *The Book Buyer*, described his poster work:

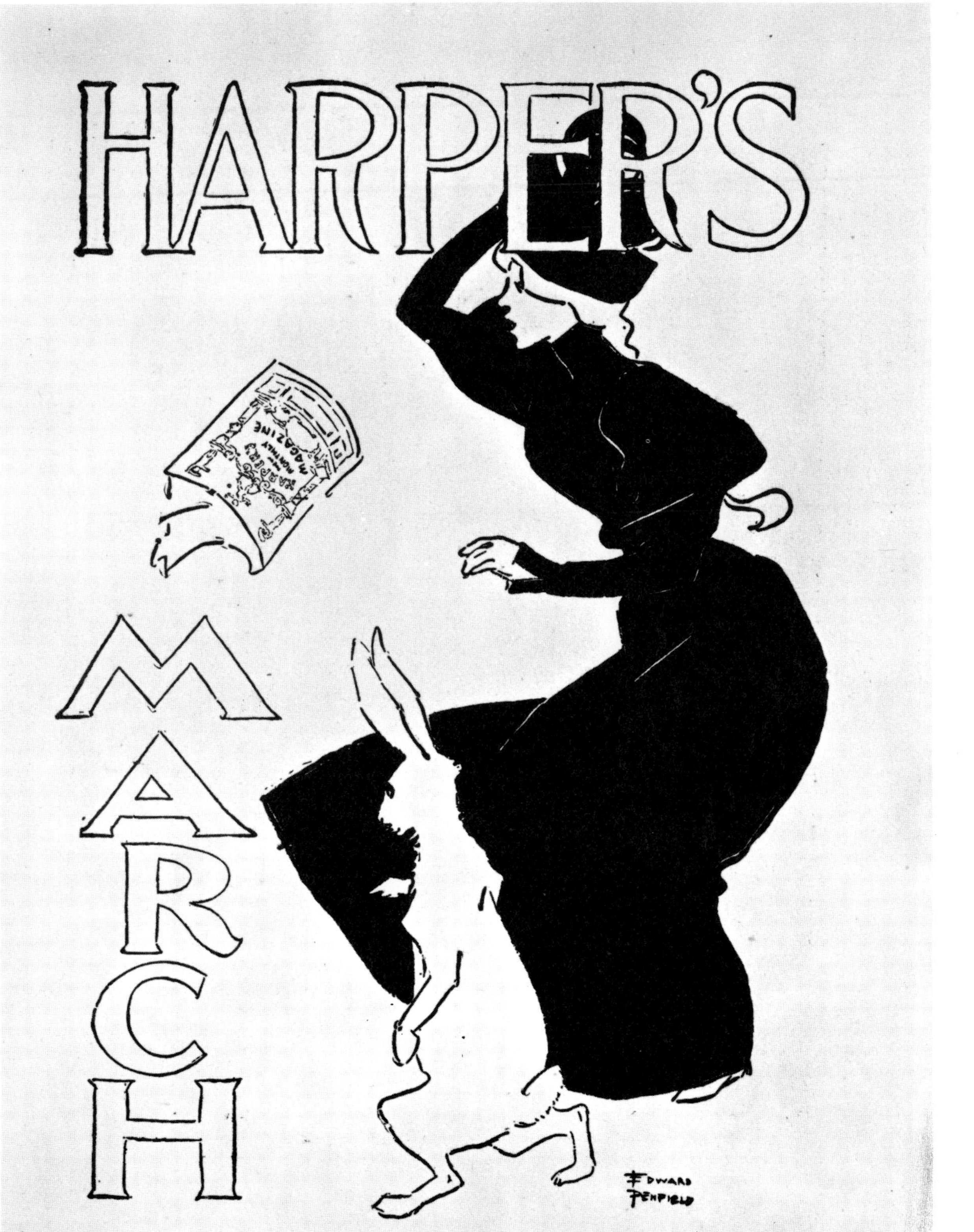
HARPER'S
MARCH
EDWARD PENFIELD

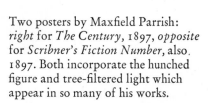

Two posters by Maxfield Parrish:
right for *The Century*, 1897, *opposite*
for *Scribner's Fiction Number*, also.
1897. Both incorporate the hunched
figure and tree-filtered light which
appear in so many of his works.

That he has unusual ability as a decorative artist has been shown
plainly during the past two or three years by the number of prizes he
has won in competition. Many will recall his beautiful and very
original drawings for the posters of the August numbers of the
Century and *Scribner's*, the former a prize-winner; the prize poster
for the Pope Manufacturing Company, won over nearly a thousand
competitors; and he who walks or rides about New York may see high
up on the hoardings another prize-winner in the shape of a hearty and
jolly looking little boy who has found contentment in a big bowl of
oatmeal. In the same line may be named several striking covers made
for the Harper's publications and the beautifully coloured design for
the December *Scribner's*.

SCRIBNER'S

FICTION NVMBER · AVGVST

Louis Rhead, poster advertising a collection of his own designs.

opposite Poster by Rhead advertising an exhibition of his unpublished posters in Paris, 1897.

Like Scotson-Clark, Louis Rhead was an Englishman by birth who achieved his poster success in America; although his first posters were produced in England, for *Cassell's Magazine*, *The Weekly Dispatch* and (it sounds like a product invented by P.G. Wodehouse) Abbott's 'Phiteesi' Boots. In America, his main work was for the *New York Sun*, the *Morning Journal*, *The Journal*, *Scribner's*, *The Century* and the *Boston Transcript*.

He was born at Wedgwood's, Etruria, Staffordshire. His father was an artist at the pottery factory, his brother a well-known member of the English Society of Painter-Etchers. When only thirteen, he was sent to Paris to study under Boulanger, and later entered the Schools at South Kensington. He next visited America at the invitation of Messrs Appleton, the publishers, and eventually settled there altogether. It was a visit to Paris and an acquaintanceship with Grasset, that started him on poster work – and Grasset's influence is strong in his posters.

opposite Louis Rhead was an uneven artist: but in this poster for *The Sun*, 1895, the Art Nouveau style and eccentric lettering are welded into a powerful design.

below Louis Rhead, poster for Lundborg's perfumes.

SCRIBNERS FOR XMAS

LOUIS RHEAD

Ethel Reed, a self-portrait in the Beardsley manner. Though slightly idealized, the portrayal, as the photograph above shows, is very honest.

opposite Louis Rhead, poster for *Scribner's*.

Parrish fails as a posterist because, although an expressive artist, he cannot adapt his detailed technique for the hoardings. Rhead is exactly the opposite: he knows quite well what an effective poster should be, but he is too inept a draughtsman to produce it himself. W. S. Rogers wrote: 'A blemish in all Mr Rhead's designs is the drawing, which in some is lamentably weak, and in others positively faulty.' Perhaps his two most successful designs are one for James Pyle's 'Pearline', and another for a June issue of *The Century*, with a tangle of yellow roses in the path of a woman reading the magazine. An article on Rhead in *The Artist* of 1896 commented:

We should not care to see all London posted by Mr Rhead. It is decoration carried as near to the boundary of affectation as possible. The cleverness lies in resisting temptation to step across the border – as Mr Aubrey Beardsley notably has done, and Mr Dudley Hardy certainly has not – in his best work. Mr Rhead is an admirable artist, but not a genius. We admire his work, and go away without the bitterness of having an irresistible longing to possess it.

Folly or Saintliness
José Echegaray

Lamson·Wolffe·and Co
Boston and New York

HELIOTYPE. PTG. CO. ~ BOSTON

HE is most truly fair to-day,
He said, who stood beside his
    horse,
Ready to mount but looking back
To where she stood upon the steps,
Crowned by an overhanging vine
Whose purple clusters touched her hair.
She must be very fair, he mused,
And then he glanced at her and saw
Her slender figure, clad in white,

Ethel Reed: *opposite* a poster for
Jose Echegaray's *Folly or Saintliness*;
right one of her illustrations to *A Book
of Fairy Tales*, published by Lamson,
Wolffe and Co. of Boston.

Ethel Reed, a handsome woman shown in *Bradley: His Book*
in a splendid picture hat, was very much School-of-Bradley, or
School-of-Beardsley, or both. Though usually competent, her
drawings and poster designs do not quite attain the mastery of
either of the Bs; but in her day she was a marvel to everyone, as
a woman who had made it in a male preserve. Bradley begins
his article on her, rather patronisingly: 'It is worth noting that
so far the so-called "poster movement" has brought into first
prominence but one woman designer. Whether this is due to a
defect in the ordinary course of training for artistic purposes,
from which young women students too seldom have the courage
to break away, or is owing altogether to the lack of original
inventiveness which women themselves evince, it would be hard
to say.' That 'Miss Ethel Reed, of Boston' had chosen to be a
posterist was all the more remarkable when one considered that

she had begun her artistic training as 'a protégée of Miss Laura Hill, the accomplished miniature painter'.

Bradley's account continued:

She has already furnished several posters to Boston publishing houses, and has, besides, illustrated various books. Book illustration is indeed her serious aim, and she is now in London busied with volumes entrusted to her erratic talent, among them a book of children's stories for Lamson, Wolffe & Co., and a second number of the delightful Yellow Haired Library series gotten out by Copeland and Day, the first number of which is 'The Arabella and Araminta Stories'. The illustrations are conceived in a true poster spirit, and while grotesque and Japanesy, have a strong feeling for childhood.

An article in *The Poster* of November, 1898 also made reference to the Japanese element in Ethel Reed's work: 'Miss Reed uses floral motives in the same way as the Japanese, and the figures of the women created by her are as sweet, if not sweeter than the fragrant flowers surrounding them.' But in the posters, that sweetness tends to be just a bit cloying: one need only compare the blowzy composition of her poster for *Miss Träumerei* ('Albert Morris Bagby's New Novel') with Beardsley's design for Singer pianos, to appreciate her limitations. The 'Träumerei' poster was produced by Lamson, Wolffe, & Co., who monopolized Ethel Reed rather as Harper's did Penfield and the 'Chap Book' Bradley. *The Poster* admired her designs for Mabel F. Blodgett's *Fairy Tales* (singularly weak drawing with terrible pseudo-gothic lettering), her 'The White Wampum' and 'The House in the Trees'; but the poster which has at any rate most historical interest, that for Le Gallienne's 'The Quest of the Golden Girl', a ravishing *fin-de-siècle* design in black, grey and gold (Whistler's influence?) they dismiss as 'the least successful of Miss Reed's works, being too complicated, and in this respect resembling the plot of the novel itself'. *The Poster,* too, like Bradley, took occasion to deliver a squashing little homily on the proper place of women: 'One can understand that women have no originality of thought, and that literature and music have no feminine character, but surely women know how to observe, and what they see is quite different from that which men see ... Strictly speaking, woman only has the right to practise the system of the impressionist, she herself can limit her efforts and translate her impressions and recompense the superficial by her incomparable charm, her fine grace, and her sweetness.' This extraordinary way of thinking persisted until the First World War, when posters appealed for women to lend their impressionist charm to the auxiliary forces and to making munitions.

opposite O. Giannini, an extraordinary poster of 1895 for the Turner Brass Works, anticipating 'Op Art' by seventy years.

Ethel Reed, poster for Albert Morris Bagley's novel, *Miss Träumerei*, 1895.

The Turner Brass Works

GIANNINI 95

Europe to 1914

'Ape-like agility in the imitation of that which, while it may be ingeniously burlesqued, cannot be honestly reproduced.' This was the verdict of that master of literary lucubration, Edgar Wenlock, on the late nineteenth-century Belgian posterists. He must mainly have had in mind the obvious derivative element in the posters of Privat-Livemont, the leading Belgian master, whose designs appear to be modelled on those of Mucha. Privat-Livemont's compatriots, who were anxious to suggest the development of a distinctive Belgian school, rejected the idea that he was a mere *pasticheur:* writing in *The Poster* of August to September, 1898, Emile de Linge said:

It has been insinuated that Privat-Livemont was a continuator, or rather an imitator, of Mucha. Such an absurd legend we distinctly deny. Livemont is an artist ever seeking for original ideals, a lover of his art, and so sure of his own powers that he can rely on himself for inspiration.

This opinion was echoed by W. S. Rogers in *The Book of the Poster* (1901), who said:

He has often been referred to as an imitator of Mucha, but a careful examination of his work will assure any unbiassed critic that the only things he and Mucha have in common are an intense passion for the beautiful, fertile invention in the elaboration of the accessory ornament – the decorative instinct – and a splendid draughtsmanship, to which must be added a mastery of colour.

But Wenlock, always on the outlook for a subject which would exercise his powers of polemic, was not so easily placated. In *The Poster* of December, 1900, he wrote:

I am no thick-and-thin admirer of the work of Privat-Livemont, nor of that of Mucha upon whom he has very obviously founded his style. Both of these artists have invented very beautiful things, but it seems to me that internal decoration, rather than street advertisement, is the field in which their talent would have its fullest scope. As an advertiser, Privat-Livemont is to be preferred to Mucha. Less exquisite, less ingenious than the Hungarian designer, his work is bolder and his colour contrasts more effective. On no hoarding could his huge poster for 'Rajah Teas and Coffees' be overlooked.

Wenlock's view is not unfair. Now that jingoist jealousies, at any rate that between England and Belgium, have disappeared, we can accept that Privat-Livemont's work, though based on Mucha's and less distinguished as pure art, probably made a greater impact on the hoardings.

Privat-Livemont was born in Schaerbeek, near Brussels, in 1861. Like so many other budding artists, he met with opposition from parents obsessed with 'security'; but at the age of thirteen, he was allowed to enter the drawing school of St Josse, where he

opposite Privat-Livemont: poster for Rajah tea, 1900. The strength and rich idiosyncrasy of this design refute the common charge that Livemont was merely an imitator of Mucha.

Imp. Lith. VAN LEER, Amsterdam.

Cette Affiche ne peut être vendue.

Privat-Livemont, from a photograph reproduced in *The Poster* magazine of August, 1898.

opposite It was quite a coup for Sidney Ransom to get Privat-Livemont to design a cover for the English magazine, *The Poster*. This is the composition he sent in, which was used for the October, 1898 issue.

studied design under Hendricks and Bourson, decoration under Gerard Kestens. In 1882 he began three years' study in the Paris art schools at the expense of the Belgian Government. After this, he worked with Lavaster, the scenic artist for the Opéra. After two years in Lavaster's studio, he left for the studio of another scenery painter, Duvigneau of the Comédie-Française. Then he moved over to interior decorating, working with several good Paris firms. In 1889 he returned to Belgium, where he took work with a Brussels firm of decorators. In 1890 he opened his own studio.

He continued with interior decorating work, and in the 1890s designed a frieze for a local government centre at Hasselt and decorative panels showing 'the feminine arts' in the Maison de Blanc at Brussels. He became one of the founder members of the 'Cercle Artistique de Schaerbeek' and it was through a competition held by the society for designing a poster to advertise their first exhibition, that he became enthusiastic about poster work. By 1895 he was a prolific posterist. His second poster was a design for *La Réforme*, a Belgian journal – W. S. Rogers condemns it for its 'ghastliness', as it shows a cloth-capped *ouvrier* in the act of stabbing a girl, her Art Nouveau tresses artistically disposed in the foreground. Other designs followed for 'l'Absinthe Robette', 'Le Savon Cristel', 'le Bec Auer', 'le Biscuit Victoria', 'le Chocolat Delacre', 'le Cacao Van Houten', 'le Bitter Oriental', 'la Plage de Cabourg', 'l'Exposition de Bruxelles, 1897', 'les Corsets Dutoit', and in 1898 an announcement for the 'Fêtes Communales de la Ville de Bruxelles'. But perhaps his best design is the one which even Wenlock had to single out for praise – that for 'Rajah Teas and Coffees', 'a glowing and insistent mass of colour'.

A design for Rajah also shows at its best the work of another Belgian posterist, Henri Meunier. The design, of an Eastern girl sniffing ecstatically the ribbon-like fumes of Rajah tea, marks a transition between the complex Art Nouveau poster and the more concentrated styles developed in Germany, especially, in the early twentieth century. The lettering has been specially invented to harmonize with the subject: the word 'Rajah' alone is shown in sinuous Arabian-nights characters like performing serpents undulating to the thin music of a fakir's pipe. His design for 'Le Pays', showing a corpse floating in water, is described by Rogers as 'a relapse into morbid sensationalism', but was acclaimed by H. Bowra in *The Poster* for July 1898:

In the design for 'Le Pays', Henri Meunier gives us a striking difference to the work of Privat-Livemont. Without any ulterior decorations, he has given us a picture at once attractive, interesting

Privat-Livemont, poster for Cabourg, 1896. The curled-paper effect of the waves was probably derived from Hokusai's famous print, 'The Wave'.

opposite *opposite* Henri Meunier: the sun-rays and mast and rigging in this design for the Casino de Blankenberghe, 1896, all lead the eye to the lettering.

and beautiful. No details mar the striking simplicity of the figure, thus making more marvellous the ghastly expression of the wan-faced corpse, who, with finger-nails embedded in his chest, floats on the surface of a sea painted in flat green, that adds to the pallor of the pain-striken features. Had the artist attempted the slightest modelling of the visage, much of the power and beauty would have been killed.

The Art Nouveau of Privat-Livemont's and Meunier's posters was rigorously controlled: the cover which Privat-Livemont was induced to design for *The Poster* in 1898 is typical. There is a kind of inevitability to the patterning, calculated logic in its very asymmetry. But another Brussels artist, Fernand Toussant, deployed Art Nouveau in an absolutely freehand style. His poster for the Café Jacqmotte gives at least the impression of happy arbitrariness, and the freedom of the lettering – a version of the old smoke-ring trick – anticipates that of modern 'psychedelic' posters. While the smoke patterns in Mucha's design for Job cigarette papers could almost be used to prove Euclidian theorems, Toussant's are wayward and emotional; the woman holding the cup, too, is no alabaster madonna.

Among the younger Belgian posterists, the most successful was Victor Mignot, born in Brussels in 1872. He began as a book illustrator; at the age of nineteen, he persuaded a Brussels publisher, Bossut, to let him undertake the illustration of a new magazine, *Le Cycliste Belge*. This paper did not last long, but in 1893 Mignot issued his own sporting magazine. His first poster appeared two years later – 'Le Cénacle', advertising a theatre of shadowgraphs run by a group of Belgian artists. Then he took first prize in a competition to design a poster for the Brussels 'Kermesse' or fair. As his early background had been in sports illustration, he naturally obtained commissions for advertising motor cars and bicycles: one design illustrated in *The Poster* of August, 1900, for Record cycles, showed 'a *fin-de-siècle* mother on her bicycle, and in the background a typical continental nurse, rather afraid of the acrobatic feat of the new woman kissing her baby.' Another design advertised the fencing school of De Bar, with two amateurs performing an assault-at-arms. Mignot also designed posters for the 'Tramways Electriques d'Ostende-littoral', for 'la Libre Critique', 'Les Affiches d'Art, atelier Paul Verdussen', 'Le Champagne Berthon', the cover of the Paris weekly *Cocorico*, 'Le Sillon' and the 'Ligue Patriotique contre l'Alcoolisme'. Mignot's gift is not so much for good draughtsmanship or colour, but for a general *joie de vivre* that he manages to infuse into the most unpromising subjects. His transport posters are alive with action: in 'Le Cyclodrome', one girl in bloomers is leaping on to her *bicyclette*, while two others in a motor-car are outraging a passer-by in driving past at

CASINO de BLANKENBERGHE.
OUVERTURE
1er JUIN
HENRI MEUNIER
1896
LITH. J. E. GOOSSENS, BRUXs LILLE.

breakneck speed with no male escort, clutching their great feathered hats to their heads, their scarves streaming in the wind.

All these artists were either born in Brussels, or lived there. But there was also a strong Liège school of posterists. The mustachio'd and bulging-eyed young men who comprised it are pictured in a *Poster* article of April, 1899: Berchmans, Rassenfosse, and Donnay. They were protégés of the publisher August Bénard, who commissioned them to illustrate his books and pamphlets and to design his posters. Colour did not seem to matter much to these Walloon artists: they were quite happy to show the main motif in black against a plain red background, as in Berchmans's poster for the Fine Art and General Insurance Company of Brussels. Rassenfosse and Donnay also designed posters for this firm: Rassenfosse's shows a naked woman holding a sculptured Athenian head; Donnay's combines two insurance risks by a thief's hands struggling to open a jewel case against a background of red flames. Rassenfosse, as the preciousness of his design suggests, was a pupil of Félicien Rops, who was also a posterist. Rops was born in 1833 at Namur, Flanders, where his parents had settled after leaving their native Hungary. In his early career, he was influenced by the lithographic work of Gavarni. His illustrations in *Uylenspiegel* and *Contes Brabançons* show this influence. Then he left Belgium for Paris, where he became a friend of Banville and Baudelaire, and later, of Barbey d'Aurevilly, Villiers de l'Isle-Adam and J. Péladan, the symbolists. His favoured subjects in painting – Satanism and death – would not have recommended themselves to W. S. Rogers. He designed only three posters: one to announce the publication of *Légendes Flamandes* by Charles de Coster, another for the brothers Dandoy, photographers at Spa, the third never published as its composition shocked the censors.

A *Poster* reporter who visited Amsterdam in June, 1898, said: 'I feel somewhat of a huntsman at a season when good game is scarce'. All the same, he was able to record that posters had greatly improved in the last few years, and his day's 'bag' included a good silhouette design for Simplex bicycles ('The Sport for All Classes') by 'H. N.' which gave the writer a chance for a little sport of another kind:

There they go, the officer taking the lead (with the serious consciousness of becoming a Commander-in-Chief some day), the new woman (although not in bloomers) following up quickly, the young sportsman, the country yokel advanced in years and the postman in the rear – people of all degrees knowing the value of their iron steeds, and speeding to their different destinations – some on pleasure, some on business. The artist shows himself to be an efficient draughtsman, and the types are well-chosen, especially the Dutch country yokel,

HOLLÄNDISCHE KU

VOM 20 MAI BIS 2 AUGUS

STAUSSTELLUNG
ᴎ KREFELD
903 IM KAISER WILHELM=MUSEUM

who is a good pronounced 'Boer', with the good-for-nothing expression his class usually wear; the fertile flat Lowland intersected by ditches, with a village in the background, renders a good idea of the 'Noord-Hollandsche' landscape ... By a simplicity of manner with a charming sunset effect, he has succeeded in giving an attractive picture in two colours – yellow and blue.

But by a year later, two men were being acknowledged as the leaders of the Dutch school: J. G. van Caspel, and Willy Sluiter. Van Caspel was born in Amsterdam in 1870. He was forced to study for the Bar until he was twenty, when at last his parents allowed him to follow his own inclination and become a student at the Amsterdam Academy of Art, under the direction of Professor Allebé. After taking first prize in the Willink van Collen competition for young artists, he left Allebé and studied in a private studio under Dysselhof, Breitner, Jacob van Lory and Van der Valck. He graduated from portrait painting and the design of large figures to interior decoration. He was commissioned to decorate the Vriessiveem Company's committee room, the Palais Royal Hotel, the Monopole Hotel, the Nieuwe Muziekhandel and the Oporto Bar in Amsterdam. While working on the last, a small saloon bar, he met Schuver, the managing director of the Senefelder Printing Company (formerly Amand's Printing Company) of Amsterdam, who persuaded him to take up poster work. His first poster, for Ilinde Bicycles, brought him the offer of several poster commissions, but he refused to leave the Senefelder Company. His next poster was for Maypole Soap, which was reproduced in different countries, the letterpress being printed in several languages. Among his best later works were those for Bakker's Oil and Blacking, Délicatesse Tea, Dutch Skate Cocoa, the General Fire Guarantee Company of Amsterdam, the General Life Insurance Company, New Rapid Cycles, Boas Chase Tyres, Iven's Photo Materials, Selten's Incandescent Gas Light Company, Halderich's Tinned Goods, Van Houten's Cocoa and Chocolate, and the Coronation Calendar for 1898. Another effective design was for the *Hollandsche Revue*, representing a well-known Amsterdam rendezvous, the reading room at Krasnapolsky's. When the Senefelder Company moved into new premises in 1897, Van Caspel was made artistic director. He designed the firm an attractive trade-mark, showing lithographers at work. He himself always drew his own designs on the stone, and, as he was in charge of the lithographic department, he was able to supervise the preparation of colour stones. He always used living models for his figures, who usually look pensive or even startled as they hold up steaming cups of Délicatesse tea or Van Houten cocoa, as though they have been trapped in front of the lens of an Ivens and Company camera: Van Caspel

opposite Berchmans's poster for the Fine Art and General Insurance Company of Brussels, 1896, is typical of the work of the Liège school.

Jan Toorop, poster for Delftsche Slaolie salad dressing, 1895: 'Toorop began with a blank shape which was then filled with sinuous linear designs.'

evidently did not see the point of a radiant Chéret smile. The manner of his posters, though unmistakeably Art Nouveau, has little in common with either French or German versions of that style. The nearest parallel to the quaint concentric motifs in which he imprisoned his figures is the revived 'Celtic' styles of England and Ireland – there is a touch of the Tara Brooch in them.

Celtic influence is also apparent in the work of two other Dutch masters, Jan Toorop and Johan Thorn Prikker, and their work, by one of the curious unvicious circles of art history, influenced the Glasgow school of Charles Rennie Mackintosh and Margaret Macdonald, who in turn were to influence the artists of the Wiener Werkstätte. Toorop took his symbolist theories from Maeterlinck; but his motifs – the hair-obsession found also in Rossetti, Mucha and the plot of Debussy's *Pelléas et Mélisande* – have more in common with the less cerebral Pre-Raphaelism. Charles Ricketts suggested that Toorop began with a blank shape which was then filled with sinuous linear designs. Certainly this seems to have been the method of his poster for Delftsche Slaolie (a salad dressing) of 1895, which was chosen as the cover design for a recent book on Art Nouveau, as quintessential of that style. Thorn Prikker, born ten years later than Toorop in 1868, has a similar, though more contorted style, seen at its most effective in his 1899 poster for the monthly review *L'Art Appliqué*, printed in Haarlem. Neither man just dabbled in poster work: it was an important part of their *oeuvre*. Both visited Germany, and Thorn Prikker spent much of his working life there. Their influence is discernible in the work of the early Art Nouveau German posterists.

In Germany, as in France, the poster was to be a favourite vehicle for Art Nouveau. The style was first disseminated there through *avant-garde* journals, and the posters advertising these are in some cases masterpieces both as posters and as exercises in Art Nouveau. In 1895 the magazine *Pan* was founded in Berlin by Julius Meier-Graefe and Otto Julius Bierbaum: for this, Josef Sattler (1867–1931) designed a superb bill, the letters sprouting as etiolated, tendril-like growths from the scroll-like leaves of a lotus, while a blue satyr leers over a sunset horizon. In 1896 the journal *Die Jugend* – from which *Jugendstil*, the German word for Art Nouveau, was derived – was founded in Munich: Fritz Dannenberg designed a poster for it, of a girl in red tights and blouse astride a champagne bottle. In the same year *Simplicissimus* was begun, and in 1896 and 1897, posters of a new brutal simplification were designed by Thomas Theodor Heine (1867–1948), the political cartoonist. Other Art Nouveau magazines which inspired good posters were *Deutsche Kunst und*

top Otto Fischer, poster for *Die Alte Stadt,* a commercial
and artistic exhibition at Dresden, 1896.

bottom Fries, poster for the A. B. G. Café, Berlin.

Thomas Theodor Heine, poster for the German magazine *Simplicissimus*, 1896.

Another Heine design – 'Die rote Bulldogge' – for *Simplicissimus*, 1897.

I. R. Witzel, poster for the illustrated magazine *Deutsche Kunst und Dekoration*, Munich, 1898.

E. R. Weiss, poster for *Die Insel*, 1899.

Dekoration, which was founded at Darmstadt in 1897; the Berlin paper *Sturm*, for which Oskar Kokoschka rather later designed a placard; *Die Insel*, which Emil Rudolf Weiss (1875–1942) launched with a strong Celtic-style poster in 1899; and the Austrian *Ver Sacrum*, which commandeered the talents of the Viennese Secessionists.

Berlin and Munich were the centres of German poster art. In a sense, this is surprising, because Berlin at any rate had no famous art schools, no immediate traditions in art. But in other ways it was the cultural centre of the country; its theatres, concert halls and exhibitions provided posterists with commissions. In Berlin, the Steglitz studio, a 'workshop for artistic printed matter' was set up in 1900 by Fritz Hellmuth Ehmcke (1878–1965) and Friedrich Wilhelm Kleukens (b. 1878). Both men were insistent on the prime importance of effective lettering in posters, and Ehmcke's bills usually consist of little else. Prominent among the Berlin posterists were Lucian Bernhard, Ernst Deutsch, Edmund Edel, Hans Rudi Erdt, Julius Gipkens, Julius Klinger, Stefan Krotowsky and Paul Scheurich. Joseph Steiner worked there before and after the First World War, and Jupp Wiertz (1888–1939) attended the arts-and-crafts school, where he was a pupil of Eugen Klinkenberg and later of Ernst Neumann. In Munich, there was a similar studio, to which Bruno Paul (b. 1874) belonged. Another Munich artist was Franz von Stuck

Jo Steiner, poster for Senta Söneland, 1912.

opposite top
Jupp Wiertz: although Wiertz has adopted an Art Deco style, he still represents the product (Kaloderma soap) entirely naturalistically in this poster of 1927. In this respect, it marks no advance on Hassall's 1898 poster for Colman's Mustard.
opposite bottom
Julius Klinger: design for Palm cigars, 1906. A perfect example of integrated lettering: the message is the dominant element in the poster.

Franz von Stuck, poster for the
'Internationale Kunstausstellung',
Munich, 1913.

opposite Henri van de Velde's only
poster – a superb exercise in Art
Nouveau – Tropon, 1897.

(1863–1928) who studied at the Munich Academy and became a
pupil of Lindenschmidt. Both men contributed to *Die Jugend.*
There was also a flourishing artistic colony in Darmstadt, where
Peter Behrens spent seven years. Henri van de Velde, the theo-
retician of Art Nouveau, only designed one poster – that for
Tropon (1897) – but as director of the Kunstgewerbliche Seminar
at Weimar, founded in 1901, he was able to influence a generation of young posterists.

The cardinal objective of Art Nouveau, at least, of the kind of
Art Nouveau enunciated by van de Velde in his series of con-
tentious essays *Les Formules,* was an end to the old bourgeois
snobberies which had established a kind of apartheid for crafts,
industrial or applied arts, palisading them off from the 'fine' arts.
This meant a new elevation of small domestic arts – furniture,
stained glass, book-binding – and of small industrial or commercial arts, including the mass-produced, soiled-by-commerce
art of the poster. There was nothing now to stop artists who
wanted to put into currency the most recondite concepts of

TROPON.

es

L'ALIMENT
LE PLVS,
CONCENTRÉ

opposite Ludwig Hohlwein, poster for
the Munich Zoological Gardens, 1912.

below E. M. Lilien, poster
for Berliner Tageblatt.

symbolism from adopting the poster as their medium; nothing to stop landscapists with a social conscience from regaling a huge public with their melting sunsets and nude-infested pastorales. It was in Vienna, of all places, with its oppressive baroque and rococo traditions, that this new social altruism in the arts, leading back to William Morris and forward to the Bauhaus, found its most enthusiastic acceptance. The Vienna Exhibition of 1873 had shown how far Austria-Hungary had caught up with France and Britain in art and industry. But by 1880–90, the masterful Renaissance revival styles of the 1860s were stale. The counter-movement against its played-out historicism was led by young and socially conscious groups of artists. In Vienna, the architect Otto Wagner declared 'a new birth of artistic creation'. An artists' society was formed, the Secession of April 1897. In March 1898 it held its first exhibition, and in November of that year opened an exhibition building designed by Joseph Maria Olbrich. In 1898, too, its members published a manifesto, based on the theories of van de Velde, in their paper *Ver Sacrum*. Art, they said, should have a social purpose, should influence the way of life of the whole population. The domestic and industrial arts should be raised to the same level as the traditional 'liberal arts'. In accordance with these theories, Arthur von Scala, appointed in 1897 as director of the Austrian Museum of Art and Industry, bought contemporary furnishings as museum exhibits. In the first exhibition of the Secessionists, there was a *Ver Sacrum* room, completely designed by Josef Hoffmann. In the Paris Exhibition of 1900, the Secessionists showed their new art to the world.

Josef Hoffmann, best known for his Palais Stoclet, Brussels (1905–11), was the founder, with Koloman Moser, of the Wiener Werkstätte. In early 1900 he had written to Felician von Myrbach, who was planning a visit to England, asking him to go and see the Guild of Handicraft of C. R. Ashbee. At Essex House, East London, Ashbee had set up a workshop where profits were shared among the craftsmen. Hoffmann also visited this colony. Works from the Ashbee *atelier* were shown at the eighth Secession exhibition of August 1901, which concentrated on interior design. Among the other exhibitors were Charles Rennie Mackintosh and Margaret Macdonald of the austere Glasgow school, Henri van de Velde and the Maison Moderne of Paris. Mackintosh designed the music room of Fritz Wärndorfer's house in Vienna, of which the dining room was Hoffmann's work; and when the 'Wiener Werkstätte-Produktiv-Gemeinschaft von Kunsthandwerkern in Wien' was set up in June 1903, it was with capital provided by Wärndorfer. Hoffmann and Moser were the artistic directors. The 'house style' owed much to the example of Ashbee and the Glasgow school; the move had really begun

opposite Koloman Moser, 'Jacob and Joseph Kohn, Furniture Fabric', 1908, signed with monogram.

АКЦ.О̄ВˢО̄
ФАБРИКИ
ВѢНСКОЙ
МЕБЕЛИ : **ЯКОВА и ІОСИФА·КОНЪ** ВЪ
НОВОРАДОМСКѢ

ГЛАВНЫЕ СКЛАДЫ ВЪ :

МОСКВѢ, СТ ПЕТЕРБУРГѢ, ВАРШАВѢ, КІЕВѢ, РОСТОВѢ Н/Д.

МЕБЕЛЬ ДЛЯ РЕСТОРАНОВЪ
КОНЦЕРТНЫХЪ ЗАЛЪ И ТЕАТРОВЪ.
ПОЛНЫЯ ОБСТАНОВКИ СПАЛЕНЪ,
СТОЛОВЫХЪ, КАБИНЕТОВЪ И ГОСТИННЫХЪ.
СОБСТВЕННЫЯ МАСТЕРСКІЯ ПОДЪ РУКОВОДСТВОМЪ
ВЫДАЮЩИХСЯ ЗАГРАНИЧНЫХЪ ХУДОЖНИКОВЪ.

PHALA...

1. AUSSTEL...

VON WERKEN DER MALERGI · PLASTIK · ARCHITECTVR · GR...
ERØFFNUNG: 1s. AVGVST_SCHLVS...

JAHRESKARTE: M. 7.—   GEØFFNET: TÄGLICH VON 9–6 U...
BEIKARTE: M. 3.—   TAGESKARTE: M. 0.50.

A masterly poster by Kandinsky of
1901, which already shows a breaking
away from Art Nouveau and into the
simplified geometry of the future
Bauhaus style.

Oskar Kokoschka, poster for the
Kunstsalon, Wolfsberg, Zurich, 1923
(with self-portrait). This copy is an
artist's proof, signed by hand and
inscribed 'o.k.'.

Egon Schiele, self-portrait in yellow
and black – an undated work.

away from the linear hysteria and swooning decadence of Art
Nouveau towards the logic and dynamic geometry of Art Deco.
The posterists of the Werkstätte (they were, of course, also adept
in many other art forms) worked in modified expressionist and
cubist styles, with typography usually dominant and always
lucid. Gustav Klimt (1862–1918), President of the Wiener
Secession in 1897, introduced the kaleidoscopic patterning so
familiar in his paintings. Carl Otto Czeschka (1878–1960), who,
like Klimt, had studied at the Vienna School of Arts and Crafts,
almost converted the letters themselves into abstract motifs. The
younger designers included Egon Schiele (1890–1918); Oskar
Kokoschka (b. 1886), among whose posters is the purple, pink

and death-white design for *Der Sturm* (1911); and Dagobert
Peche, who designed some delicate typographical posters for the
Austrian Museum for Crafts and Industry.

Jules Benczur, director of the Hungarian Academy of Painting at Budapest, designed a poster for the 1885 Budapest exhibition. But it was not until 1896 that an Hungarian posterist
of outstanding talent appeared, when Arpad Basch produced
designs to celebrate the one thousandth anniversary of the foun-
dation of the Hungarian kingdom. At that time he was only 23,
and fresh from a training in Vienna and Paris. Three years later,
he was an international poster celebrity. *The Poster* in England
published an article on him and other Hungarian posterists,

Arpad Basch, the Hungarian posterist, in his studio.

Drawing by Arpad Basch: 'the finicking virtuosity of his linear style, delightful in a programme or menu design, would be lost on the hoardings.'

illustrated by a photograph of Basch in his studio, a bearded, jowly man built on Mucha lines, as were many of his poster designs. Among his commissions were posters for Kühnee of Budapest, agricultural engineers, and for Fahrrad bicycles (a cyclist drawn by a stag). But like Mucha, Basch sometimes draws too well to achieve an effective poster. The finicking virtuosity of his linear style, delightful in a programme or menu design, would be lost on the hoardings. Other Hungarian posterists, without Basch's artistic pretensions or the inhibitions of a Paris training, could produce bills as powerful as John de Vaszary's 'Bem Petöfi' or the advertisement for Brazay's embrocation which won first prize in a poster competition organized by the Hungarian arts-and-crafts journal *Iparmuveszet*.

Gavarni's biographer, Octave Uzanne, said of nineteenth-century Spanish posters that they were no more than 'omelettes of oranges'. But he was referring to the traditional bullfight posters, with their plethora of scrambled motifs, and not to the new wave of French-influenced Spanish posters of the 1890s. Because of the practice of advertising bullfights, there was a long pre-history of poster design in Spain; and in the 1890s when poster collectors were looking for antecedents to contemporary posters, a lot was written about these early bills. The earliest surviving was a letterpress-only placard of 1782, with its courtly statement that 'The authorities allow spectators sitting in the sun to let down one brim of their hats, so as to obviate the inconvenience caused by the sunlight'. Later, wood-cut illustrations

This poster for Brazay's embrocation
won first prize in a poster competition
organized by the Hungarian magazine
Iparmuveszet.

An exquisite design by the Spanish posterist Alejandro de Riquer, 1898.

opposite 'Granja Avicola de Sn. Luis', a poster of 1896 by de Riquer.

were added, and after the 1830s lithographic posters were produced, with graphic scenes of disembowelled horses, lance-poniarded bulls and matadors clambering up poles. Some were designed by Daniel Urrabieta Vierge, the black-and-white master, in the 1860s. With the introduction of chromo-lithography, poster design ran wild, with an indescribable hotch-potch of lettering at different angles, with figures, arches, animals, formal motifs and scarlet gore splattered all over the design like coloured scraps on a Victorian screen.

The new school of Spanish posterists developed, significantly, in Catalonia (of which the capital city is Barcelona – in the 1890s the artistic centre of Spain): for Catalonia stretches along the southern frontier of France. There is no doubt of the French influence on the work of the pioneer of this school, Alejandro de Riquer. As with Privat-Livemont in Belgium and Basch in Hungary, the main inspiration comes from Mucha, although de Riquer was also influenced by Eugène Grasset's work, which had been a model for Mucha himself. De Riquer was one of those

A Spanish *fin-de-siècle* poster by A. Sual for Cosmopolis cycles.

opposite Giovanni Mataloni: a design for the Auer Gas Mantles Company, 1895. At this period the allegorical-mythological figure was very popular in Italian posters, especially for mundane products like gas mantles, difficult to depict as romantic in themselves.

fairly formidable dilettantes who were to the Belle Epoque what the *uomo universale* was to the Italian Renaissance. He had travelled in France, England and Italy; he was a *littérateur* and published a memoir of his childhood, *Quan jo era noy*, illustrated with vignettes by himself; he made his name as a landscape painter in the goose-girl style of Val Prinsep, and as a book illustrator he executed fine stained-glass windows and frescoes for the monastery of Monserrat. An article on him by Maurice Demeur in *The Poster* of January, 1899, tells us that 'His models all belong to the English Pre-Raphaelite School of which he is an enthusiastic admirer'. His first poster was for his own memoir; but it was only after the design of his posters for 'Granja Avicola de Sn. Luis' and for the Exhibition of Arts and Crafts in Barcelona, that the orders began to pour in. He was at his best in designs for jewel shops or romantic novels which gave scope for the mysterious, mosaically stylized design he had adapted from Mucha and Grasset.

The other side of French poster style – the free handling of Chéret and Lautrec – was the chief stimulus to the work of de Riquer's friend and rival Ramon Casas, art editor of the Catalonian weekly *Pel and Ploma*. His posters for aniseed brandy (Anis del Mono) – women in Spanish national dress accepting noggins of liquor from marmosets – show that the Chéret-Lautrec style was more naturally adapted to the Spanish genius than the cool, hierophantic abstractions of the Grasset-Mucha axis. The monkeys, incidentally, were the trade-mark of Anis del Mono; an English writer, C. Street, in *The Poster* of November 1899, felt it necessary to reassure his readers:

It is, however, to be understood that the monkey is regarded more affectionately in Spain, and if you wish to please a doting parent you have only to call her child a monkey (*mono*) which is the highest compliment your vocabulary can afford.

When all has been said in favour of the national character of Belgian or Spanish posters, one has to admit that they rarely rose to the level of the *affiches* of the French masters, and never excelled them. But in Italy at the same period, there were a few designers who developed styles of their own and whose best works can challenge the French on their own terms. The Italian poster scene was dominated by the publishing firm of Ricordi (Milan) and the group of artists it employed. The company had been founded in 1808 by Giovanni Ricordi and Felice Festa. Ricordi went to Germany to study the latest developments in engraving. He brought back the newest printing press and its inventor, Josef de Werz. Later he sent his son to Germany to learn the techniques of lithography. Giulio Ricordi also went to Paris to

opposite Adolfo Hohenstein: this poster for Puccini's *Tosca* was one of the early opera designs published by the Ricordi company.

LA STRAGE DEGLI INNOCENTI
ORATORIO DI D.ON LORENZO PEROSI
G·RICORDI&C·EDITORI

F. Laskoff, poster for Perosi's
La Strage degli Innocenti.

opposite Mataloni, poster for *L'Ora,*
1900.

learn photo-engraving. He was the first to introduce into Italy the 'offset' machines for monochrome or several colours, and to use the lithographic technique to reproduce originals in colour. The photolithographic illustration of Manzoni's novel *I Promessi Sposi* in 1828 showed what could be achieved, although Manzoni was furious about the reproductions and had the first copies of the book withdrawn from circulation.

By the 1880s, Ricordi were best known as music publishers; they had a branch in Regent Street, London, as well as in Milan. One of their biggest commissions was to print opera scores and to advertise opera performances by posters. In 1889, Ricordi's first poster designers – Mataloni, Hohenstein, Metlicovitz – were given the job of planning this publicity. Adolfo Hohenstein, born in St Petersburg in 1854 of German parents, designed a

L'ORA

GIORNALE POLITICO QUOTIDIANO
DI PALERMO - DIRETTORE: AVV.
VINCENZO MORELLO (RASTIGNAC)

L'ORA AVRÀ IL PIÙ VASTO SERVIZIO TELE-
GRAFICO, DIRETTO, DA TUTTE LE CAPITALI D'EU-
ROPA.

L'ORA AVRÀ, OLTRE QUELLA LOCALE DI
PALERMO, UNA REDAZIONE SPECIALE A ROMA
E UN MINUTO ED AMPIO SERVIZIO TELEGRA-
FICO, PER LA CRONACA, LA DISCUSSIONE E
TRATTAZIONE DI TUTTE LE QUESTIONI POLITICHE.

L'ORA AVRÀ ILLUSTRAZIONI QUOTIDIANE.

L'ORA AVRÀ LA COLLABORAZIONE LETTE-
RARIA ORDINARIA DI GABRIELE D'ANNUNZIO,
MATILDE SERAO, ENRICO PANZACCHI, LUIGI
CAPUANA.

ABBONAMENTI
ANNO — SEMESTRE — TRIMESTRE
IN PALERMO - L.22.— L.11.— L.5. 50
NEL REGNO — "24.— "12.— "6.
ALL' ESTERO — "40.— "20.— "10.
UN NUMERO CENT.mi 5 IN TUTTA ITALIA
DIREZIONE E AMMINISTRAZIONE:
PALERMO - VIA CINTORINAI 62.

Marcello Dudovich: this 1911 poster for Borsalino hats shows a rare early use of still-life in the poster.

poster for Puccini's *Edgar* in 1889; in 1895 he produced a bill for *La Bohème;* and in 1899, his best-known dramatic design for *Tosca.* Leopoldo Metlicovitz (1868–1944) was the designer of another Puccini opera poster, *Madame Butterfly* (1904): his design was a straight crib from a Japanese print by Hiroshige, but Hohenstein's design for the same opera, also in 1904, is both more enterprising in the choice of scene, and more orthodox typographically.

In Italy, the new pictorial posters made the same kind of impression on a public used to letterpress only, as Chéret's had made in France. Vittorio Pica describes his first encounter with a poster by Mataloni in the streets of Naples (December 1895): '... rallegrava con un inattesco sorriso d'arte la tristezza di quella grigia giornata piovosa d'inverno. Lieto oltremodo della gioconda sorpresa mi avviciai al bel cartellone e rimasi a lungo a contemplare la vaga fanciulla, il cui fiorente corpo giovanile appariva in tutta la sua leggiadria dietro un sottile velo nero.' ('... it cheered with an unexpected artistic gaiety the gloom of that rainy, grey winter's day. So extraordinarily thrilled was I at the joyous surprise that I went up to the fine poster and long contemplated the insubstantial girl whose budding youthful body appeared in all its grace behind a thin black veil.')

Some of the posters of this period are allegorical or idealized, like Mataloni's 1898 design for Cora vermouth, which shows an elegant national-costumed peasant-girl with a wicker basket of grapes, gazing moodily into the middle distance. But most of them show contemporary life, certainly the more glamorous side of it, the Campari culture, but naturally, spontaneously, and faithfully. The children advertising clothes by E. and A. Mele & Company of Naples, in Aleardo Villa's poster of 1896, look as if they have been caught in a casual snapshot: the girl, in her frilly mob-cap, red jacket and high buttoned boots is shy and winsome, the boy in his sailor suit and spat-boots grins past the camera as if sizing up a target for his catapult. Villa (b. 1865) committed suicide in 1906. His posters for the Mele stores, who were among Ricordi's best clients, all give the same impression – that the artist is spying on one instant in time, catching a fashionable woman gloating over a box of kid gloves before deciding which pair to chose for the evening; or a nattily dressed man, cane and hat in hand, bending down to kiss a white-gloved hand, or a girl in an Easter bonnet, not staring the viewer out with an air-hostess beam, but looking wistfully to one side.

Metlicovitz also designed a number of posters for Mele of Naples. Of all the Ricordi posterists, he gives the most delightful portrait of the Italian Belle Epoque; in a poster advertising Mele's clothes for women, he inks in minutely the paste brooch

LA RINASCENTE
·MILANO·TORINO·GENOVA·BOLOGNA·FIRENZE·ROMA·
·NAPOLI·BARI·PALERMO·

opposite Leopoldo Metlicovitz: poster of 1913 for 'La Rinascente' clothes shop. Unlike Dudovich, Metlicovitz associates the product with its market.

on the woman's feathered hat; the white dragon-style embroideries on her violet dress; the frills on her salmon-pink parasol. But this model, who must have answered all the store's requirements, is set against an enchanting sunlit background, in which more parasols are grouped like a colony of coloured minarets in front of an expanse of olive sea on which boats are racing. His poster for the Varese shoe factory has a similarly impressionist quality.

Marcello Dudovich (1878–1962) was a pupil of Metlicovitz, and many of his posters – for Mele children's clothes, Liquore Strega, Uliveto or the Motoring Club of Milan – have the same devil-may-care lightness. But the poster with which he won a competition organized by the Borzalino Company in 1910 has been described by Attilio Rossi in these almost metaphysical terms:

It actually anticipates the so-called 'poster-object' later theorized by the German, L. Bernard. In fact, in that dominant and unusual yellow light that invades the entire poster, the 'still-life' of the article to be advertised, the black bowler hat, becomes inseparable protagonist, while the armchair, the gloves and the stick recite *sotto voce* their subordinate role to the distinction and courtliness of the product.

This hymn to a bowler hat could almost make one reject Monneret de Villard's more sober pronouncement on the Italian poster in his 1914 introduction to a portfolio of seventy Ricordi posters: 'It has been one of the most genuine products of our time.'

Hans Rudi Erdt, poster for Rotkäppchen, 1912.

Auskunft-Erteilung und Speditions-Uebernahme
durch
W. G. TAAKS G. m. b. H., CREFELD.

ERÖFFNUNGSFEIER DES SIMPLON-TUNNELS
INTERNATIONALE AUSSTELLUNG
MAILAND - 1906
APRIL - NOVEMBER

From the Great War to 1939

In an essay on eighteenth-century Spain, Professor Hugh Trevor-Roper has spoken of the 'Oriental immobility' of the Spaniards. The phrase represents one extreme of the attitude traditionally ascribed to the Eastern mind, that of deprecating the new. The corresponding trait attributed to the Western mind (notably, of course, by Westerners) is 'a restless scientific curiosity', which, at its least admirable extreme, means too great an openness to the new – including propaganda.

Branding hemispheres and races in this way is an inexact, some would say, a pernicious science. No one could accuse modern Japan of imperviousness to new ideas, or modern China of immunity to propaganda. But a study of European history does leave one with an uncomfortable impression that the West has tended, with an almost systematic perversity, to give credence to the false and to spurn the true. For example, when Marco Polo wrote of his travels in Cathay, he was put down as a romancer, and his book became known as *il milione* from the million marvels (or lies) it was believed to contain. When he was on his death bed, pious relations begged him to save his soul by confessing how often he had been guilty of invention in the book, 'to which his reply was that he had not told one half of what he had really seen'. Yet Polo's book was basically true; while *The Travels of Sir John Mandeville*, a medieval best-seller accepted for some two hundred years as the most reliable authority on the Orient, was later exposed as based merely on hearsay. Sir John Mandeville had never existed: the author of the travels was a Frenchman who had never ventured further than the Mediterranean.

There is a parallel in the two world wars. As Mr A. J. P. Taylor puts it, in a footnote to his *English History, 1914–45*: 'In the First World War nearly everyone believed the stories of German atrocities, though relatively few were true. In the Second World War nearly everyone refused to believe the stories, though they were true, and the German crimes the most atrocious ever committed by a civilized nation.'

The 'atrocity' stories of the First World War were the material for some of the most vicious posters ever produced. One of these stories was first given currency in the *Dumfries Standard* of 16 September 1914, only a month after the outbreak of war. It described how a Dumfries nurse, Grace Hume, aged twenty-three, had had her breasts cut off by German soldiers who had burnt down the Vilvorde Camp Hospital and left her to die in agony. The story was backed by a letter from another nurse, Nurse Mullard, who had been with her at her death. Only after this story had been headlined in the national papers, was it found that Nurse Hume was still in England on the staff of the

opposite David Wilson, First World War 'atrocity' poster.

RED CROSS OR IRON CROSS?

WOUNDED AND A PRISONER
OUR SOLDIER CRIES FOR WATER.

THE GERMAN "SISTER"
POURS IT ON THE GROUND BEFORE HIS EYES.

THERE IS NO WOMAN IN BRITAIN
WHO WOULD DO IT.

THERE IS NO WOMAN IN BRITAIN
WHO WILL FORGET IT.

THE DANGERFIELD PRINTING CO. LTD. LONDON.

BRITAIN·NEEDS YOU·AT·ONCE

PUBLISHED BY THE PARLIAMENTARY RECRUITING COMMITTEE, LONDON. POSTER Nº 124.   PRINTED BY SPOTTISWOODE & CO LTD LONDON E.C.

right and opposite Both sides prayed
to the same God to send them victory;
and both invoked the traditional
dragon-slaying heroes of their lands.

Huddersfield Hospital, and that Nurse Mullard had never
existed. The whole story was made up by Nurse Hume's younger
sister Kate, a hysterical girl of seventeen who was later brought
to court. By now, the story had seized the imagination of the
public, who were in the mood to be shocked, and of the British
and American propagandists, who found it a suitably horrifying
basis for poster and pamphlet attacks on German inhumanity,
even though they could no longer in this case, as with Edith
Cavell, name names. A typical design shows a moronically
beaming German soldier, wearing iron crosses labelled 'Murder'
and 'Ruin', ripping the allies' flags while the bloodied naked
bodies of a woman and her baby lie in the background.

Chopped-off breasts were rather too indelicate for British,
French or Belgian hoardings; but there was great exploitation
of the equally unsubstantiated reports of chopped-off hands. *The*

1914 ——— 1917

Zeichnet die Sechste
Kriegsanleihe

Times had published a dispatch early in the war from its Paris Correspondent, reporting that 'an official of the Catholic Society' had recently interviewed a man who 'had seen with his own eyes German soldiery chop off the arms of a baby which clung to its mother's skirts.' On 2 May 1915, the *Sunday Chronicle* told how 'a charitable great lady' was visiting a home for Belgian refugees in Paris when she noticed a little girl of ten whose hands were hidden 'in a pitiful little worn muff'. When the child asked her mother to blow her nose for her, the great lady suggested she was old enough to blow her own, and was told by the mother: 'She has not any hands now, ma'am.' The stories were packed with circumstantial detail, such as Captain Marryat might have invented to give plausibility to one of his children's novels; but no facts were given. A French poster by Gallo shows a German in a spiked Hindenburg helmet, his eyes wild with bloodlust, triumphantly holding aloft the severed hands of a girl who is lying among field flowers, his bayoneted rifle resting on her body. An American recruiting poster, headed 'They Mutilate', shows the statue of 'Kultur' in front of a blazing city – a blind, handless Belgian child on a plinth. 'For Humanity's Sake, Enlist' is the slogan beneath. Women were included in the composite image of the beastly Hun: an English poster shows a German 'sister' pouring water on the ground in front of a British soldier crying out for it. 'There is no woman in Britain who would do it,' the poster says. 'There is no woman in Britain who will forget it.' The poster is headed 'Red Cross or Iron Cross?'.

The crucified Canadian was another popular theme, always good for a shudder of moral fury. The story was published in *The Times* of 10 May 1915: wounded Canadians had been forced to watch one of their officers crucified – 'He was pinned to a wall with bayonets through his hands and feet and then another bayonet was driven through his throat.' Even at this distance of time, the thing sounds real; in fact it was just another fabrication. The subject was illustrated in a poster of Goyaesque horror by D. G. Widhopff. An infinitely sad Christ appears in a bright nimbus to kiss the cheek of the screaming, hollow-eyed soldier, pinned with huge nails to what looks like a stable door. 'Frère ...' breathes the Saviour. The design was entitled 'Hommage à la maman du Canadien crucifié, 1915'.

But it would be wrong to lay too much emphasis on these sensational and vitriolic canards. They were only a minute fraction of a mass of bills mainly designed for more mundane purposes than inflaming national tempers. For these other posters – recruiting, fund-raising, morale-boosting – a subtler and calmer approach was favoured, though in a way this was almost as tendentious as the propaganda based on 'atrocity'

opposite J. C. Leyendecker, First World War poster for USA bonds.

228

U·S·A BONDS
Be prepared
Third
Liberty Loan
Campaign
BOY SCOUTS
OF AMERICA
WEAPONS FOR LIBERTY

THE
MOTOR·CORPS
OF
AMERICA

Howard Chandler Christy: poster to
recruit women volunteers for the
Motor Corps of America, 1918.

stories. Realism, of the kind that Brangwyn could have offered if he had been invited to design more than the few posters Frank Pick commissioned from him, was out. Death was to be sold like Bovril, with nice, healthy, cheerful placards. Efficient censorship in all the combatant countries generally managed to keep out of the Press the Armageddal casualty figures, the unpalatable realities of life in the trenches. The posterists, too, were advised not to show the 'seamy' side of warfare. One way of glamour-izing it was to adopt an allegorical-heroic approach. All countries produced posters of St George and very parfit gentil knights polishing off dragons of varying repulsiveness. German posterists also favoured Valhallan heroes with shaggy blond beards, Brunhildes in full career (the English had Boadicea), and latter-day Siegfrieds. The United States conscripted a starry-eyed Statue of Liberty – she appears behind the sword-bearing boy scout in J. C. Leyendecker's poster for USA Bonds and in Joseph Pennell's Liberty Bonds poster which showed what it would be like if New York came under air raid attack: Liberty's sun-ray head has been blasted off and lies in a heap of rubble at the foot of the pedestal. France had the Phrygian-bonneted figure of Liberty, usually a deal more voluptuous and realistic than other nations' allegorical heroines. She materializes serenely in the background of a poster by Lucien Jonas, sprinkling Liberation Loan over charging soldiers from a golden cornucopia. Even more reassuring and cosy were the posters by Francisque Poulbot, previously best known for his *bourgeois-risqué* urinating urchins ('Buvez jamais de l'eau') – the idyll of the piddle. In his 'Soldier's Day' poster, he showed a small boy dressed as a soldier (continent for once) and his sister as a Red Cross nurse, pleading pathet-ically for contributions 'Pour que papa vienne en permission, s'il vous plaît' (so that daddy can come home on leave, please). Even a poster which has been praised for its unflinching realism, the magnificently drawn French soldier of Jules Abel Faivre's National Defence Loan poster ('On les aura!' – we'll get 'em!) is a romantically idealized figure. No one with any sense of survival ever charged the enemy with one hand raised in flamboyant salute.

At the beginning of the war, recruiting posters were the obvious necessity, especially in England, where full-scale con-scription was not introduced for a year and a half. Probably the most successful, and certainly the most imitated, was the 'Your Country Needs YOU' design by Alfred Leete, with the relentless pointing finger of Lord Kitchener. It began life as the cover of the weekly journal *London Opinion*. It gave Lloyd George the material for one of his sarcastic quips: 'Kitchener,' he observed, 'is a great poster.' Only pacifists could jib at the tone of the

"BE HONEST WITH
YOURSELF. BE CERTAIN
THAT YOUR SO-CALLED
REASON IS NOT A
SELFISH EXCUSE"
LORD KITCHENER

ENLIST TO-DAY

With its bold silhouette effect, this recruitment poster signed by V. Soutril was one of the most artistically satisfying of the First World War.

Leete poster; but other methods of poster recruitment were more dubious. One way of suggesting that a man was cowardly if he did not volunteer was to get at him through his children and womenfolk. 'Daddy, what did YOU do in the Great War?' a sheepish father is asked in Savile Lumley's design, by the small girl on his knee, while his son disconsolately plays with the toy soldiers and miniature cannon on the carpet. 'Women of Britain say – GO' is the caption of E. V. Kealey's design: an Eton-cropped woman, her arm round her evening-wrapped daughter, small son tugging at her dress, nobly watches out of the window as a company marches off. In its most pointed form, the message was printed simply in bold letterpress on a poster that read:

To the YOUNG WOMEN OF LONDON. Is your 'Best Boy' wearing Khaki? If not don't YOU think he should be? If he does not think that you and your country are worth fighting for – do you think he is WORTHY of you? Don't pity the girl who is alone – her young man is probably a soldier – fighting for her and her country – and for YOU. If your young man neglects his duty to his King and Country, the time may come when he will neglect YOU. Think it over – then ask him to JOIN THE ARMY TO-DAY.

The mentality which issued this kind of stuff was that which also led young women to stand outside men's lavatories offering white feathers to those entering or emerging who were not wearing uniform. This kind of moral blackmail caused a number of suicides among medically unfit men who had been rejected for the services. But the lowest point of enlistment advertising was surely reached in the anonymous British poster which appealed to self interest, with a view of a zeppelin over the dome of St Paul's and the wonderfully specious caption: 'It is far better to face the bullets than to be killed at home by a bomb'. The further caption with which the poster conventionally signs off – 'God Save the King' – could almost be interpreted as a cynical aside. If, by contrast, one had to choose the best enlistment poster, it might be Norman Lindsay's Australian design, with the simple caption 'Fall-in!' brave in white on black, the picture being a marching column of Australian soldiers, their webbing and water-bottles forming a white criss-cross pattern against the bright ochre of battledress. Or, although the ethics are again in question, one cannot deny the powerful impact of Fred Spear's American poster, 'Enlist' – the scene here being a mother and her child drowning in fishy green fathoms, an allusion to the sinking of the *Lusitania* (1915) in which a thousand civilians, including a hundred and twenty-eight Americans, had died.

The leading American posterists in the First World War were Howard Chandler Christy, Babcock Dressler, James Montgomery Flagg and Charles Dana Gibson. Maxfield Parrish, too, turned his petit-point technique to the subjects for which it was least suited – tanks, battleships and anti-aircraft guns. He would have been better employed in portraying a winsome girl in Motor

Daddy, what did **YOU** do in the Great War?

PUBLISHED BY THE PARLIAMENTARY RECRUITING COMMITTEE, LONDON. POSTER NO. 79.　　　　DESIGNED AND PRINTED BY JOHNSON, RIDDLE & CO., LTD., LONDON, S.E.

The nadir of the poster caption in England: an anonymous poster issued by Pat Posters in the Great War.

opposite Savile Lumley, 'Daddy, what did you do in the Great War?' The poster was printed by Johnson, Riddle and Company.

Corps of America uniform, the subject which in fact fell to the stronger and more dashing treatment of H. C. Christy. The best-known of the American wartime posterists was Charles Dana Gibson – creator of the famous 'Gibson girl'. His posters pilloried profiteers and slackers, and encouraged soldiers, housewives and 'farmerettes'. He was also a master of heart-wrenching. One of his posters, captioned 'Here he is, sir', shows a mother offering Uncle Sam her young son. Gibson's son Langhorne posed for the boy, and later followed the poster's action: he left Yale as soon as he was old enough to enlist and served on a destroyer in the latter months of the war. A photograph in Fairfax Downey's 1936 biography of Gibson shows him at work on one of the 90 by 25 feet canvases that were set up in front of the New York Public Library to attract crowds and promote Liberty Loan

235

drives. Artists such as Gibson, Charley Falls, N. C. Wyeth and
Henry Reuterdahl, working from outlines previously blocked in,
painted figures representing the various branches of the Service
and the Allies.

Wallace Irwin, looking back on the achievements of the
Division of Pictorial Publicity, celebrated them with some
occasional verse:

THOUGHTS INSPIRED BY A WAR-TIME BILLBOARD

I stand by a fence on a peaceable street
And gaze on the posters in colours of flame,
Historical documents, sheet upon sheet,
Of our share in the war ere the armistice came.

And I think of Art as a Lady-at-Arms;
She's a studio character most people say,
With a feminine trick of displaying her charms
In a manner to puzzle the ignorant lay.

But now as I study that row upon row
Of wind-blown engravings I feel satisfaction
Deep down in my star-spangled heart, for I know
How Art put on khaki and went into action.

There are posters for drives – now triumphantly o'er –
I look with a smile reminiscently fond,
As mobilized Fishers and Christys implore
In a feminine voice, 'Win the War – Buy a Bond!'

Charles Livingston Bull in marine composition
Exhorts us to Hooverize (portrait of bass).
Jack Sheridan tells us the Food's Ammunition –
We've all tackled war biscuits under that class.

There's the Christy Girl wishing that she was a boy,
There's Leyendecker coaling for Garfield in jeans,
There's the Montie Flagg Guy with an air of fierce joy
Inviting the public to Tell the Marines.

And the noble Six Thousand – they count up to that –
Are marshalled before me in battered review.
They have uttered a thought that is All in One Hat
In infinite shadings of red, white and blue.

And if brave Uncle Sam – Dana Gibson, please bow –
Has called for our labours as never before,
Let him stand in salute in acknowledgement now
Of the fighters that trooped from the studio door.

No war in history had ever brought civilians into the arena of warfare to such an extent; and this gave force to the many appeals for funds which followed the recruitment posters. These ranged from the Christopher Robin baby-charm of 'God Bless Daddy Who Is Fighting the Hun – and Send Him Help!' to the open savagery of Frank Brangwyn's view of a German being bayoneted: 'Put Strength into the Final Blow – Buy War Bonds'. The Germans used the same slogan beneath a more mythological hero smiting the British lion with a two-edged sword: 'Es gibt die letzten Schlage, den Sieg zu vollenden – Zeichnet Kriegs-anleihe!' Then there was the inevitable appeal for help for the wounded, for orphans and for prisoners-of-war. These posters were the most dignified and moving, because they enjoined compassion to the unfortunate, not terror to the iniquitous. A British poster signed 'L.B.', for the Machine Gun Corps Prisoners of War Fund, shows a man weeping in a cell. Its pathos is only rivalled by Hönich's poster of a weeping German family: 'Farmers, do your duty: the towns are hungry!'. The figure of the mother, her face entirely hidden by a gnarled hand, has the emotional authority of a Van Gogh drawing.

It is strange, in retrospect, to follow the development of artists who before the war had never had to design anything more heart-wrenching than an advertisement for cocoa powder. The professional posterists who had made their names in the 1890s found it difficult to adapt their styles to the requirements of war propaganda. John Hassall, perhaps, was happy enough designing a bill for the Public Schools Brigade (Royal Fusiliers 118th infantry brigade): he had drawn the football-togged prefect figure for the cover of *The Captain* magazine, and the only slightly older boy in khaki drill who waves his cap in the air and exhorts his friends: 'Hurry up! Boys – Fill the Ranks' might be the same prefect a year later. There were others, such as Steinlen, whose style had always been rather too emotionally charged for everyday product advertising. These now came into their own, and in his posters for *L'Aisne Devastée* (for the reconstruction of destroyed homes), for *Journée Serbe* (Serbia Day) and above all in the poster in which he condemned the Germans for letting Russian prisoners starve ('Sur la Terre Ennemie Les Prisonniers Russes Meurent de Faim'), with its Dostoyevskian, sunken-eyed couple, he was producing work as good as he had ever done. But Adolphe Willette's draughts-manship seems to have got even worse by the time of his Red Cross poster of 1916, and there is not much to be said for the veteran Edward Penfield's 'Will You Help the Women of France' poster, urging Americans to save wheat: there is little variation on the rather static, although decorative, manner of his Harper's advertisements of the '90s.

But the First World War did bring into prominence three great German posterists: Ludwig Hohlwein, Lucian Bernhard, and Julius Gipkens. All three had an extreme economy of style and a preference for the silhouette technique – the nearest earlier parallel is the work of the Beggarstaff brothers. Hohlwein was born in Wiesbaden in 1874. He studied at the technical high school in Munich and was later an assistant of Wallot in Dresden. He began poster work in 1906. By 1907, with his posters for Hermann Scherrer, the breeches-maker and sporting-tailor of Munich, his style was already formed – a style of sharp contrasts and simple, geometric lettering. By 1912, in a poster for Audi automobiles, he was taking artistic liberties that even the Beggarstaffs had never thought of: the chauffeur's check coat is divided into grey squares by a yellow chessboard pattern, quite regardless of where the folds of sleeve or lapel fall. The chassis of the car is indicated with brilliant highlighting and the most Stygian of black shadows.

Like some general who finds peacetime manoeuvres and ceremonial parades tedious but comes to life on the battlefield, Hohlwein found he was able to express the vitality and malice of his genius in his war posters. Even in the poster appealing for contributions to the Ludendorff Fund for the Disabled, he manages to suggest the frustration and powerfully repressed tensions of the crippled soldier. This tension is also conveyed by his commanding poster for the German Prisoners' Fund, oddly reminiscent of the Beggarstaff's Cinderella poster in the effect made with iron bars in the design, the great red heart on the freedom side suggesting all that the brooding prisoner, in his muffler and braces, is missing in the outside world. And again we see it in his advertisement of an exhibition of work by German internees in Switzerland: he achieves the difficult effect of misery without sentimentality, pathos without bathos.

Lucian Bernhard, born in Vienna in 1883, also studied at the Munich Academy, which became a centre of poster design. His principal talents were for lettering (a number of types were named after him) and for *mise en page*. In his pre-war posters, for Adler typewriters, Kyriazi cigarettes or Stiller shoes, he employed a form of lettering similar to that, rounded and serifed, used by the Beggarstaffs; but for his war posters, he favoured a dynamic gothic letter. With him, the slogans and captions are always the most important element, and sometimes he only gives text, as in 'Die Kartoffel rettete Deutschland!' (The potato has saved Germany). One can imagine how Hassall or Brangwyn would have interpreted the same subject, with pictures of toiling farm workers, brawny arms, beads of sweat, and healthy red children. But when Bernhard does design an

opposite Anonymous poster printed in England by David Allen and Sons shortly after the First World War.

Lucian Bernhard, poster for Osram electric-light bulbs.

opposite Lucian Bernhard, 'Die Wahrheit ins Ausland' (Spread the truth abroad). The design is perfectly integrated with the lettering, and indeed seems to take on a calligraphic character of its own, so that one almost expects to be able to read it as a collection of hieroglyphics'.

Ludwig Hohlwein, poster for the German Prisoners' Fund. 'The great red heart on the freedom side suggests all that the brooding prisoner, in his muffler and braces, is missing in the outside world.'

die Wahrheit ins Ausland!

26484

Wir versenden in Verbindung mit dem Deutschen Archiv der Weltliteratur E. V. eine Nachrichtenzeitung in 10 Sprachen an die Presse der neutralen Staaten zu kostenlosem Nachdruck. Helft uns durch Geldspenden und durch Auslandsbeziehungen!

Zuschriften sind zu richten an den Direktor des Deutschen Archivs der Weltliteratur, Dr. Hermann Beck, Berlin W 15, Schaperstraße 25, Geldsendungen an die Deutsche Bank, Depositenkasse B. C., Berlin W 50, Schaperstraße 1, für das Konto „Auslandspresse".

Neutraler Ausschuß für objektive Preßberichte nach dem Ausland:

Svend Gabe (Dänemark), A. Grenander (Schweden), G. Hassi-Bey (Türkei), J. Hissink (Holland), L. Illiesu (Rumänien), Geo. Kubler (Verein. Staat.), G. F. Marini (Italien), Ramon de Miranda é Zurbe (Spanien), H. Oroschakow (Bulgarien), Silva Pinto (Brasilien), J. Schaffner (Schweiz), Th. Slenberides (Griechenland), R. Wlig (Norwegen).

HOLLERBAUM & SCHMIDT · BERLIN N 66

EN BELGIQUE
LES BELGES ONT FAIM

TOMBOLA ARTISTIQUE
au profit de
L'ALIMENTATION POPULAIRE DE BELGIQUE
CHAQUE BILLET DE
CINQ FRANCS
DONNE DROIT :

A_ à un souvenir, œuvre
spéciale: soit une gravure
du peintre FIRMIN BAES,
soit une médaille breloque
du sculpteur DEVREESE,
B_ au tirage de la tombola
des dons d'ART APPLIQUÉ.
(DENTELLES, BRODERIES,_
PEINTURES SUR VASES,_
SOIERIES, etc. TRAVAUX_
DES FEMMES BELGES)_

ON PEUT SE
PROCURER DES BILLETS
AU SIÈGE DE
L'ALLIANCE FRANCO-BELGE
58, Rue de la Victoire,
à PARIS.

PRÉSIDENTS D'HONNEUR_
DE L'ALLIANCE FRANCO-BELGE
S.E. le Baron GUILLAUME, Ministre
Plénipotentiaire de S.M.le Roi des Belges à Paris_
M. Louis BARTHOU, Député, ancien
Président du Conseil des Ministres
M. Émile VANDERVELDE,
Ministre d'Etat de Belgique_
VICE PRÉSIDENT D'HONNEUR :
M. DALIMIER, Sous-Secrétaire d'Etat
au Ministère des Beaux-Arts.
_ PRÉSIDENT :_
M. STEEG, Sénateur, ancien Ministre,

Steinlen
1915

I. LAPINA, Imp. PARIS.

Steinlen, poster in aid
of the starving
in Belgium, 1915.

illustration, as in 'Die Wahrheit ins Ausland!' (Spread the truth abroad), it is perfectly integrated with the lettering, and indeed seems to take on, like the figures in a Hokusai book, a calligraphic character of its own, so that one almost expects to be able to read it as a collection of hieroglyphics.

Gipkens, too, was born in 1883, at Leipzig. He studied at the Dresden Academy under Oehme, Preller and Starke. Gipkens is a more frivolous artist than the other two. His pre-war posters are full of neo-rococo conceits, and of cartoon scenes, such as a teddy bear lighting a gas lamp. He is capable of a more dashing simplicity than Hohlwein or Bernhard, but it is the simplicity of a *jeu d'esprit*, of colourful sketchy spontaneity, not of calculating austerity. His poster for Doyen cigarettes was probably the least cluttered that had yet appeared anywhere in Europe; and students of the history of 'pop' art who give their scholarly attention to Colin Self's hot dogs and Claes Oldenburg's hamburgers of the 1960s would do well to look at Gipkens's superb poster for Kaiser brick coal of 1913. It could almost be a photograph of a creation by Andy Warhol. A man with so ungovernable a sense of humour was not the ideal artist to express the heroic or tragic aspects of war. The German authorities wisely commissioned him, instead, to design appeals for the populace to collect acorns and chestnuts. Another poster, asking them to collect fruit stones for oil production, shows two pigeon-chested prune stones waddling purposefully along in straw hats. His more serious efforts – 'Help our heroic airmen', and so forth – are less felicitous.

In England, the two outstanding war posterists were Frank Brangwyn and G. Spencer Pryse. Both felt an especial concern for the plight of Belgium. Brangwyn had been born in Bruges (where there is now a museum of his work). Spencer Pryse's interest in Belgium is explained in a book by Martin Hardie written just after the war, in 1920:

To Mr G. Spencer Pryse belongs the honour of first realizing in actual productions the needs of the time. Mr Pryse was in Antwerp at the outbreak of war, and thus was an eye-witness of much of the tragedy which overtook Belgium. On the actual scenes of the evacuation were founded his pathetic lithograph of the Belgian refugees struggling into steamers to escape from the advancing terror. Shortly after, he obtained a commission to act as a despatch-rider for the Belgian Government, in which capacity he visited all parts of the line both in Belgium and in France, and saw a good deal of desultory fighting. Before he was wounded, he drew several of the series of nine lithographs entitled 'The Autumn Campaign, 1914', which were published early in 1915. His poster, 'The only Road for an Englishman', was of the same period, followed soon afterwards by his powerful

G. Spencer Pryse, 'The Only Road for an Englishman' – one of the posters commissioned by Frank Pick.

opposite Rex Whistler: the lightness and brilliant conceits of Whistler's murals for the Tate Gallery tearooms are reflected in this London Transport poster.

Through Darkness to Light

THE ONLY ROAD FOR AN ENGLISHMAN

Through Fighting to Triumph

THE TATE GALLERY

Weekdays 10 a.m. - 4 p.m.
Sundays 2 p.m. - 4 p.m.
Admission free *(Tuesdays and Wednesdays 6ᵈ)*

TRAFALGAR SQ. OR WESTMINSTER STN.
thence by bus 32, 51ᴬ, 80, 88, 89, 180 or 181

opposite E. McKnight Kauffer, poster for an exhibition of modern silverwork at Goldsmiths' Hall.

pictorial appeal on behalf of the Belgian Red Cross Fund. It is interesting to know that even under the most difficult conditions, and under fire, his drawings were made, not on paper, but on actual lithographic stones carried for the purpose in his motor-car.

From the First World War onwards, Frank Pick was the supreme impresario of the 'industrial arts' in England. It was he who, as general manager of the London Underground, commissioned the war posters of Brangwyn and Spencer Pryse. In 1917 he asked Edward Johnston to design a new type for Underground posters – the now famous 'Underground letter' which was the basis of the sans serif type of Johnston's pupil, Eric Gill. With his friend, the architect Charles Holden, Pick revolutionized transport architecture. He commissioned Epstein and Henry Moore to design sculptures for the new London Transport building at 55 Broadway. And he was continually introducing new talent into poster design. His most brilliant protégé was E. McKnight Kauffer, whose poster of the London Museum (1922) is one of the classics, the Old Masters, of poster design. Kauffer chose as subject the Fire of London (of which there was a large press-button illuminated model at the Museum). He converted the amorphous flames into a flaring vorticist pattern – cubism in motion.

The London Museum poster informed its viewers that the nearest point of access by London Transport was Dover Street or St James's Park Station. This was the theme of Pick's advertising: one did not just show a train rushing through pretty scenery: one showed the destination and told people the route. Another of his successful young designers, less dynamic than Kauffer but with strength in his delicacy, was Frank Newbould, whose pastel vignettes of English scenery were sometimes accompanied by choice fragments of English verse. Percy V. Bradshaw, in his *Art and Advertising* (1925), complimented Pick on the deceptive gentleness with which he accomplished the hard sell:

Truly Mr Frank Pick deserves gratitude as the inspiring force behind what has often been described as London's most popular Art Gallery... He has mapped out delightful and economical excursions for the working-class family, he has robbed the wet Bank Holiday of its former terrors, and he has given imaginative artists a free hand in proving that Art and advertising are inseparable terms. It would be a merry experience to watch a harassed board of directors or an old-fashioned advertiser examining a dainty poster bearing the words:
    'Further afield the May still sweet,
    There are many ways out of London',
and discovering that the rest of the 'commercial appeal' and 'selling talk' on this poster consisted of the words:

'Queen Guinevere rides a-maying into the Woods and Fields
beside Westminster to great Joy and Delight.'

Can this type of pictorial adventure bear any relationship to the advertising of a railway? It *can* – and does. Poetry can be very practical.

This form of advertising was also very cheap: in 1924, Ian Fraser, publicity manager of the Underground, said that the entire yearly expenditure on posters, including the cost of their reproduction, was only £5,000. Each year, a hundred new designs were being commissioned. Some artists found the opportunities of this kind of work satisfying enough for them to forsake the wider art world above ground. In *Blasting and Bombardiering* (1937), Wyndham Lewis, the vorticist leader, wrote:

Some were very anxious indeed that we should do a bit of 'blasting' again. They pressed me, as a born leader in such affairs, to up and 'blast' a way for them through the bourgeois barrage. And at length I thought I would. I founded 'X Group'. After a short while I left this Group and it fell to pieces ...

One of 'X Group's' most prominent members was MacKnight [*sic*] Kauffeur [*sic*], who became the Underground poster-king: he disappeared as it were below ground, and the tunnels of the 'Tube' became thenceforth his subterranean picture galleries. I went underground too ...

The open-air railway systems were not slow to follow the example of the Underground. W. M. Teasdale, the advertisement manager of the London and North-Eastern Railway, commissioned Frank Brangwyn's poster of the Royal Border Bridge, Fred Taylor's 'Interior of York Minster' ('England's Treasure-House of Stained Glass'), Frank Newbould's 'Scarborough' and Lilian Hocknell's 'Clacton-on-Sea'. The best of his discoveries was Tom Purvis, whose posters for the East coast, of sun-bathers with parasols and belles in dinghies, show a real mastery of colour juxtaposition. Norman Wilkinson, the marine painter, suggested to the manager of the London, Midland and Scottish Railway that poster commissions should be offered to selected Royal Academicians and Associates. These included Brangwyn, D. Y. Cameron, George Clausen, Charles Sims, Sir William Orpen and Augustus John. Maurice Greiffenhagen, whose poster for the *Pall Mall Budget* (1893) was one of the earliest to introduce the new French style into England (D. H. Lawrence modelled his artistic style on him more than any other painter), now reneged on that early freedom in a taut, obsessively detailed heraldic design for 'Historic Carlisle: the Gateway to Scotland' (1924). It was suddenly discovered that everywhere, if it could not be described as the 'garden' of somewhere, was the 'gateway' to somewhere more enticing.

Charles Gesmar: one of his classic posters for Mistinguett, 1926.

Gauro: this poster of 1927 advertising Trouville seems to encapsulate the essence of Bright Young Thingery.

Austin Cooper, British Railways poster
for the London and North Eastern
Railway.

opposite Emil Preetorius, an
exhilarating poster for an exhibition
of his own work.

The shipping companies joined in the competition for poster
artists. Norman Wilkinson worked for Cunard, Austin Cooper
for Royal Mail, and Frank Newbould for Orient Lines. Dudley
Hardy and Hassall were also recruited for shipping posters, and
the latter contributed a most unalluring temptation to visit
Norway – a dim-looking peasant holding a large hayfork.

Hassall and Dudley Hardy were still in business, and there
were enough old-fashioned advertising managers to keep them
fully employed. But their basically academic, Dutch-realism or
ersatz-Chéret styles now seemed very tame beside the Art Deco
styles deriving from cubism, vorticism and the Bauhaus, and
their lettering seemed fogeyish and unimaginative compared
with the new letters developed from the typographical research
of men like Stanley Morison, Francis Meynell, Johnston and
Gill. The traditional symmetrical composition they favoured was
being rapidly outmoded by the lay-out principles of Moholy-
Nagy, who joined the Bauhaus staff in 1923: the idea of a poster
in which every inch of space would be filled with coloured design
was being superseded by an appreciation of *mise en page*, the
effective deployment of the blank space.

In Germany, as we have seen, these principles had already
been put into practice, even before the First World War, by artists
such as Hohlwein, Bernhard and Gipkens, at a time when
German expressionism in painting was in its infancy and cubism
in France was nascent. One thinks also of the posters for the
magazine *Simplicissimus* by Thomas Theodor Heine (1867–1948),
who was also one of that journal's most vituperative cartoonists;
of the exhibition posters of Emil Preetorius (b. 1883) who became
head of the Munich teaching workshops in 1910 and was later
to design Thomas Mann's bookplate; and the superbly laconic
designs of Paul Scheurich (1883–1945), whose versatility ex-
tended to the modelling of porcelain figures for the Meissen
factory, hailed by W. B. Honey in his monograph on the factory
as the best modern work to be found in ceramics. But the German
poster did not progress from this early mastery. Fritz Koch-
Gotha's 1922 poster for *Die Woche* shows no emancipation from
the rigorously formulated style of 1910; while Bernd Steiner's
Norddeutscher Lloyd poster of 1929 is actually retrograde.

It was in France that the disparate collection of influences
that made up Art Deco* found its most virtuoso, least self-
conscious expression. The leader of the French school was an
unbelievably precocious designer named Charles Gesmar, who
was born in Paris in 1900 and died there in 1928 in a scarlet

* The author has discussed what these were in *Art Deco of the 1920s and
1930s* (Studio Vista, 1968).

preetorius-
ausstel-
lung ·
p—
64 Goethestr.
Brakl's · moderne
Kunsthandlung

C. Gesmar, poster for Gilda Gray,
1925.

opposite Leon Bakst, 'Caryathis',
c. 1925. The Russian Ballet, of which
Bakst was the chief designer, was an
important influence on poster art of
the 1920s.

fever epidemic. He was already producing posters in the First
World War. A French anti-Semite was heard to say: 'That
Gesmar, if he were a Frenchman instead of a Jew, would be at
the Front fighting the Boche.' At the time, Gesmar, his posters
all over Paris, was only fifteen. At the end of the war, in 1918,
he was hired as a designer at the Folies Bergères, and became the
chief designer at the Olympia and other theatres. He designed
the costumes (this cannot have been arduous work at the Folies)
and the décor, and was also responsible for the playbills. In
1922, 1925 and 1926, he produced posters for Mistinguett, the

music-hall singer who liked to appear with a twenty-five-foot train of feathers and fifteen pounds of egret on her head. (She preserved her exotic image until the end in 1955 when, we are told, 'she lay dying for twelve days on a pink satin bed, dressed in a pink silk négligé.') The 1922 Gesmar poster shows her with one eye concealed by a rakish hat, a jungle of long green feathers sprouting from its side. In another, she has a rose clenched between her teeth. Gesmar also designed posters for Leslie and the Dolly sisters in 1922; in 1923 for Jane Marnac, who later took part in *Pluie*, an adaptation of Somerset Maugham's *Rain* at the Théâtre de la Madeleine – the subject of another famous poster by Paul Colin; in 1924 for Marguerite Cempley – one of his most spirited designs, with a bird of paradise fluttering above the actress in her mink-trimmed wrap; in 1925 for the Rowe sisters, Lucienne Delahaye, Elvire Popesco the Rumanian bombshell, Yvonne Legeay (a design strongly influenced by Van Dongen's portraits) and the Italian star Falconetti, lounging in a chaos of ostrich plumes and Fauve-coloured cushions; in 1926, for the American male performer Randall and the high-wire transvestite Barbette, the Danny la Rue of his day, dressed in nothing but a blonde wig, a huge plumed fan, and a rope of pearls around his midriff.

The influence of Gesmar's style is seen in Charles Kiffer's 1923 poster for Maurice Chevalier, who is represented as a Cheshire cat grin beneath a straw hat worn like a guard's cap; and in the kaleidoscopic shimmer of Gauro's 1927 poster for Trouville, in which the blazered and white-flannelled mashers and the swimming-hatted girls epitomize Bright Young Thingery. Other artists took a more literal lesson from cubism, among them Jean Carlu, whose design for Larrañaga cigars, for Crawford's Advertising Company, could almost, without the lettering, be taken for a Picasso collage. The best of the hard-edge men was 'Cassandre' (Adolphe Jean-Marie Mouron). He was born in the Ukraine of French parents. He first made his name in Paris in 1923 with his poster 'au Bucheron'. His design for Dubonnet – 'Dubo ... Dubon ... Dubonnet', with a little cubist man in a bowler hat gradually being suffused by the red apéritif, was adopted by the firm as their trade-mark. His masterpiece is his 1927 poster for the *Etoile du Nord* – the railway service linking Amsterdam and Paris by a coalition between the Chemin de Fer du Nord, the Société Nationale des Chemins de Fer Belges, and the Nederlandsche Spoorwegen. There is no sex, no charming scene of bosky dells and waterfalls, not even a romantic express hurtling past. It is simply a ruthlessly reduced abstract design, of silvery railway lines converging on a star, the lettering set against subtly harmonizing violet and ochre.

Kees van Dongen, poster of Arletty, 1931. At that time Arletty was appearing in the Revue de Rip at the Théâtre du Palais Royal. She was born Léonie de Bathiat, and the stages of her career were factory girl, typist, model, cabaret artist, film star.

top Ludwig Hohlwein, poster for the German Olympic Games, 1936.
bottom Poster for Dubonnet by 'Cassandre' (Adolphe Jean-Marie Mouron), 1932.

'Cassandre's' masterpiece:
the Etoile du Nord
poster of 1927.

opposite A. E. Marty: typical of the posters Frank Pick
commissioned for London Transport, this idyllic design
of 1931 is captioned with a few lines of poetry, nothing else.

"Where runs the river? who can say
Who hath not followed all the way
By alders green and sedges grey
And blossoms blue?"

By

VINCENT BROOKS, DAY & SON, LTD. LITH. LONDON W.C.2.

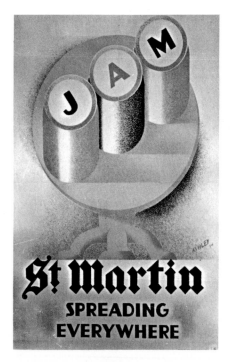

Ashley Havinden ('Ashley'), poster for St Martin jam, signed and dated 1928.

opposite Ashley Havinden's 1927 poster for Eno's Fruit Salts: 'a cunning way of dividing an unwieldy slogan into four coloured tiers.'

The Cassandre approach began to succeed the old pictorialism in England. Eno's Fruit Salts, previously advertised by a picture of a rocking galleon with the sublimely euphemistic caption 'The Gently That Does It', was replaced by Ashley Havinden's 1927 design of wild horsemen bearing on pennants the caption 'First thing every morning renew your health with Eno's Fruit Salts' – a cunning way of dividing an unwieldy slogan into four coloured tiers. Graham Sutherland (in 1932) and Paul Nash (in 1937) designed 'modernistic' landscape posters for Shell, and in 1932 Clifford and Rosemary Ellis advised people to visit Whipsnade Zoo by car using B. P. Plus. John Gilroy (b. 1898) produced his 'My Goodness, My Guinness' posters in the mid-thirties. But two of the most expanding industries of the '20s and '30s – motor cars and motion pictures – still tended to prefer the straight pictorial advertising that showed the man in the street just what he would be getting for his money. Codognato's Italian poster of 1925 for the Fiat 509 showed a cable-thewed centaur holding aloft the car: the centaur is indicated in outline, but the car is drawn with photographic realism. In Hincklein's 1925 German poster for Dunlop balloon cord tyres, one can even read the lettering on the tyre edge. Rudolph Valentino as the Eternal Lover, and Ronald Colman as Clive of India might be idealized, suburban dreams made flesh, but the posters were still illusionist: the viewer was meant to accept the ideal as fact.

Simple men did accept the poster ideal as fact in the Spanish Civil War (1936–9), in which both sides made heavy use of poster propaganda. Claud Cockburn says in his autobiography:

When I ... joined this same Fifth Army as a private and went to the Sierra Front with a company of barely trained peasants, the first time we went into action ... a lot of the men charged holding their rifles high above their heads with one hand and giving the clenched first salute with the other.

It emerged that they had taken the highly stylized and symbolical posters designed by the Madrid intellectuals, showing a Soldier of the Republic in this posture, as illustrations of correct military practice.

When they saw me dodging along, bent half-double and taking whatever cover there was, they thought the posture unworthy, despicable. A lot of them were killed or wounded before they got converted to the idea that, as instructional diagrams, there was something wrong with those posters.

Nothing could better illustrate the power of the poster than this macabre anecdote of men flinging themselves into death at its suggestion. By the Second World War, radio had become the principal instrument of propaganda, but still no country could ignore the primitive graphic appeal of the propaganda poster.

opposite Bernd Steiner: this poster, by the artistic director of the Bremen city theatre, is a simplification of Steiner's original 1929 design with German text only.

below United Artists' Corporation, poster for the film *Clive of India*, 1935, starring Ronald Colman and Loretta Young.

The Modern Poster

Max Beerbohm's cynical observation in the 1930s that 'we need another war – to bring out the best in our artists, and to kill off the worst of them' was almost justified by the event. Ashley Havinden, one of the best wartime posterists, wrote after the war:

The war expanded the opportunities for the artist in many ways. Although with its outbreak the emphasis shifted away from preoccupation with advertising commercial products, the need for effective advertising was vital. The limitation of newspaper space naturally limited press advertising design, but in the poster field the Government realized that shouting injunctions from the hoardings in conventional designs would not have the vigour and urgency required to attract attention. The authorities must be commended for the progressive policy they followed in commissioning designers of the calibre of Tom Eckersley, OBE, FSIA; F.H.K. Henrion, MBE, FSIA, Abram Games, FSIA, Zero (Hans Schleger, FSIA); Lewitt-Him. The result was that the majority of official posters were modern vivid designs, which made their point clearly.

This was true of the posters of almost all the combatant countries. The most glaring exception was Japan. Ironically and inexplicably, the country whose *avant-garde* art had inspired the whole modern poster movement in the late nineteenth century now turned out the most feeble and pedestrian designs: the Tokyo paper the *ABC Weekly* of 4 March 1940 illustrated a poster advertising Army Day. It shows a heroic militiaman, rifle at the ready, with aeroplanes thick as crows in the sky behind; it might have been drawn by Willette in his less palmy days. The paper reported: 'The War Ministry has issued many posters like the one shown here. It has also published 120,000 pamphlets to remind people of the day.' There was only one other exciting piece of front-page news that day: 'A future grand champion *sumo* wrestler is in Fukuoka Prefecture. He is K. Minematsu by name. Though only sixteen years old, he is already five feet eight inches tall. He weighs 150 pounds.' Japanese propaganda reached a slightly more effective level, though hardly a sophisticated one, in the posters they issued urging India to cast off the European yoke and drive out the British oppressors: two muscular Indians in turbans goose-step over the wreckage of British aeroplanes, while a shifty little Englishman with a red nose, tin hat and tattered Union Jack stumbles along in flight before them.

Poster themes of the Second World War were quite different from those of the First War. There was no need for recruiting posters, as there was mass conscription. The main new themes were: careless talk costs lives (illustrated both by Abram Games's sinister bayonet design and by the more humorous approach of the *Punch* cartoonist 'Fougasse', who showed Hitler

opposite Roland Ansieau, 'Bons de la Libération à intérêt progressif', a signed work of the Second World War.

BONS
DE LA LIBÉRATION
à intérêt progressif

and Mussolini sitting behind two housewives in a bus); personal cleanliness and hygiene advertisements to prevent epidemics; 'Horse-play with weapons may end like this'; appeals for blood donors; and many suggestions that people should grow their own food – of which the best is Abram Games's design 'Use spades not ships', in which half the hull of a ship and half a pointed spade are joined together, with characteristic pictorial wit, to form a trowel-shape. A pair of stockinged feet in a jungle of ravelled wool advertised 'Our Jungle Fighters need socks'; and later on Games also produced the moving poster 'Give clothing for liberated Jewry'.

The countries still free could afford good-works posters of this kind (though not always the paper to print them on). Less altruistic posters were appearing in the occupied countries. The Vichy Government and the German occupational forces produced propaganda posters, including one of a German soldier with some French children – 'Populations abandonnées, faites confiance au soldat Allemand!' After the war, the French photographed this alongside several of the less soothing bills the Germans posted – announcements of the execution of resistance workers, promises of condign reprisals if saboteurs did not give themselves up, and the like. But the resistance made use of posters too: the Force Française Intérieure were constantly posting seditious bills printed on clandestine presses, and just a few days after the liberation, they plastered the hoardings and kiosks of Paris with the liberation poster by Paul Colin.

They also tore enemy posters down: one, showing Churchill as a hideous green octopus, was torn into pieces which, carefully preserved, have now been stuck together. The 'octopus' poster was typical of the designs which were intended to discredit the enemy simply by showing him as a monster; and here, the techniques had not become more subtle since the First World War, although now the Nazis were able to add the Communist menace to their rogues' gallery – 'Europe contre Bolchévisme', one of their occupation posters proclaims. And there was also the new Fascist racial bias: not only against Jews, but against Negro soldiers in the American army: one Nazi poster shows a Negro GI clutching the Venus de Milo, on which a large dollar sign has been painted.

In America, there were posters for national defence, for the Committee to defend America by Aiding the Allies, for Bundles for Britain and United China Reliefs. They were mostly of a low standard, but one must except 'America's Answer: Production', a design by Jean Carlu, who had come to America, and the war posters of McKnight Kauffer, who had returned there. Most of the United States Government posters appeared under the

opposite William Little, 'Keep Death off the Road', 1946. The poster was criticized in the Press as too shocking.

**KEEP DEATH
OFF THE ROAD**

CARELESSNESS KILLS

CONFIANCE...

DAKAR

MERS-EL-KÉBIR

LYBIE ÉGYPTE

imprints of the Office of Emergency Management, the War Production Board, the Office of Facts and Figures, the Office of Civilian Defense and the Office of War Information. But private industry also contributed morale-boosting designs. John Atherton (who, like Games, produced an excellent anti-gossip poster), Joseph Binder, Henry Koerner, Ben Shahn and Symeon Shimin were among the most talented designers.

There were few atrocity posters. The old half-gentlemanly days of propaganda had gone, and nations were more inclined now to boast of their own inhumanity than to pillory that of the enemy. The Germans, for example, issued a poster captioned 'Diary of Death' – the blood-soaked diary, with bullet-hole, taken from the pocket of an Allied soldier 'just like you'. A few posters showed the same degree of viciousness as First War designs, in particular an American one, 'This is the Enemy', a black gallows reflected in the monocle of a sneering Nazi officer; or Russian posters which showed Hitler and his deputies munching blood-stained bones from a trough, or alternatively, being stabbed to death by a 'Russian broom' made up of dozens of red bayonets.

One new idea introduced in England during the war was of the propaganda exhibition, in which great use was inevitably made of posters. The exhibitions branch of the Ministry of Information was headed by Milner Gray whose deputy was Misha Black. With their able designers, including Henrion, Peter Moro and Frederick Gibberd, they established exhibition techniques which continued to be used after the war, notably in the Festival of Britain in 1951, one of the few good things, artistically, to come out of the 1950s. Ashley Havinden recalls some of the wartime exhibitions in his *Advertising and the Artist* (1956): the 'London Pride' exhibition in Charing Cross station, 'Private Scrap Builds a Bomber' (salvage drive), 'Gangway Please' (war transport), 'Comrades in arms' (Russia at war), 'The Unconquerable Soul' (resistance movements in occupied countries) 'Off the ration' at the Zoo, 'Fuel exhibition' at the Dorland Hall and the dramatic army exhibition on the John Lewis bombed site, which covered 56,000 square feet with 23,000 exhibits.

The period between the end of the war and the early 1960s was an uneasy one of skirmish and compromise between photography and graphics in the poster. Already in the 1930s photography was being widely used in posters, especially by the Swiss school of designers – Alois Carigiet, Herbert Matter, Niklaus Stoecklin – who from the beginning took refuge in compromise, with admittedly very effective combinations of photographic images and graphic design. But many of the posterists who had developed individual graphic styles before the war were not prepared to have any truck with photography: this was seen as

An anonymous poster of about 1942, showing Churchill as a green octopus. It was torn down by a French Resistance worker, but later pieced together again as a relic of occupation.

opposite 'Leap Year', a decoration-only
poster published by Osiris Visions,
London, in 1968, from a photograph
by Bobby Davidson.

a surrender to that old cunning aim of the manufacturer, which the early pictorial posterists had only with difficulty managed to frustrate, to have his product illustrated in the poster with complete faithfulness. Ashley Havinden strongly put the view of the pure graphic artist in a supplement on advertising in *The Times* in 1964:

> The creative arts of the layout man and the poster designer have been sadly warped. In too much British advertising today there is now a sameness of expression: the ubiquitous 'grot' types, squared-up photographs . . . . Graphic design – and indeed the art of the poster, as we used to know it – seems to have disappeared completely from the hoardings in favour of the 'blown-up' photograph. The appeal in advertising is no longer to the intuitive or unconscious part of the mind – but to the rational forefront of it, with the stress on cupidity.

The tendency toward a photographic poster was increased by the competition of television, which brought images of products right into the home with convincing realism.

Nevertheless, because by 1945 the pure-graphics posterists were at the top of their profession, the graphic poster was not suddenly eliminated from the hoardings. In 1946, for example, William Little designed his 'Keep Death off the Road' poster ('Carelessness Kills') with a black-veiled widow staring bleakly into the middle distance. The design made its impact, and indeed caused a furore in the press as some considered it over-macabre; but if shock was the object (and it must have been) then surely a photograph of a real woman in black with a tragic expression would have more powerfully and poignantly brought home to drivers the real risk and the real suffering. Air France patronized Jean Carlu and Roger Excoffon, and the result was some telling graphic design: only later was it realized that a photograph of an aircraft in a waste of blue sky was worth a dozen 'artists' impressions'. In 1948 Raymond Savignac, one of the most respected of modern French posterists, designed a comic thermal figure with a radiator heart to accompany the caption 'Utilisez le Coke'; later advertisers have found it more effective to photograph a family in bathing costumes in a centrally-heated room with snow visible through the windows. In America, Saul Bass and Ben Shahn; in Switzerland, Donald Brun, Herbert Leupin and Karl Gerstner; in Germany Heinz Edelmann (who designed a sinister-comic poster for *The Ladykillers*) and Walter Breker; in Italy, Franco Grignani and Giovanni Pintori; in Finland, Eric Bruun and Marti Mykkanen; and in Poland, Tadeusz Trepkowski and Waldemar Swierzy, to select some representative examples, are all principally graphics men, with little dependence on photographs or photographic tricks.

This does not mean that the graphic poster did not develop. On the contrary, a rapid succession of artistic movements in Europe kept it in a state of continual flux. Surrealism was a particularly congenial influence. In 1943 Lewitt-Him designed a surrealist poster for General Stampers (Welwyn) Ltd: 'If you can't grow fingers, grow careful' – a cactus-like growth of green fingers springing up from the ground. Again, Lewitt-Him's poster for American Overseas Airlines, with its distorted watch, was obviously based on the melting watches of Salvador Dali ('The Persistence of Memory', 1931). James Gardner's loud-speaker symbol for the 'Britain can make it' exhibition may have been inspired by René Magritte's 'The Eye' (1932). Posters were enlived by the linear wit of Paul Klee, and their disparate elements sewn together by web-like mazes of lines derived from Calder's wire mobiles and Gabo's nylon-mesh structures – as in Robin Day's 'Jet' poster for the Ministry of Supply exhibition, 'Zero's' for Terylene and Herbert Leupin's for Coca-Cola. And one great artist, John Heartfield, admitted photo-montage into posters with brilliant effect.

By the late 1950s, the condition of the poster was eclecticism run wild. In his book of 1956, Ashley Havinden wrote:

To solve each problem the mature designer will draw on any period of expression, and will mix these periods if necessary – if, by so doing, the aptness, speed and conviction of communication are thereby enhanced. His sole criterion is his own good taste and artistic integrity towards his work. He feels free to draw on classical antiquity; Bauhaus functionalism; early Victorian quaintness; Surrealist dream images; candid camera snapshots; engineering blueprints; the space divisions of abstract art and modern architecture; the typography of the fifteenth century; X-ray photography; wood engravings; statistical diagrams; the new typography of Tschichold; fantastic decorated display letters, etc., etc.

Abram Games, perhaps the greatest of contemporary posterists, held a gloomy view of the prospects for poster design:

Not for nothing has the broad grin become advertising's universal symbol in post-war years. Most international posters have, in one way or another, provided this circus atmosphere, reflecting the constant and wild search for entertainment to escape from the realities of our lives. Whether the grin has now established its purpose and will gradually fade remains to be seen. Perhaps the world is now turning to face its problems more seriously ... The flowing frivolities of the grin period may be superseded by the pretty patterns of tachism or more formalized and frigid abstractions. Whether these will be more acceptable as a true expression of the times I don't know.

That was written in 1960. What *has* happened? Well, first, there has been a far more candid acceptance of the role of photo-

opposite One of an effective series of posters produced by Philips to advertise Philishave electric razors. This poster of 1968 shows how completely the photograph has taken its place in the modern poster, after so long being spurned in favour of even indifferent graphic work.

'Psychedelic' poster for the Carnaby
Street, London, boutique,
'Kleptomania'.

graphy – not just in huge blown-up pictures of the product (as
of brown, brimming tankards of Bass) but in highly imaginative compositions such as the 'foreigners' series advertising
Philishave electric razors. But secondly, pure-graphics posters
have been given a new and half-crazy life, as well as a new
status in art, by the school of 'psychedelic' poster design, some of
whose origins are in the Victoria and Albert Museum's great
Beardsley exhibition of 1964. This exhibition, together with the
Mucha exhibition of the previous year, was one of the main ingre-
dients of the Art Nouveau revival, represented by books such as

'The Dragon and George', produced by Copyrun Ltd from an original drawing by J. Pemberton. This poster of 1968 is a good example of the visual joke as decoration, for which the poster is an ideal vehicle.

Robert Schmutzler's, Maurice Rheims's and Mario Amaya's; by new fabric and book-jacket designs; and, in posters, by the delicate designs for Elliott shoes. Art Nouveau and Beardsley meant 'decadence', and it was therefore natural that the 'beautiful people' and the 'flower children' of the pop-music, drug-taking, drop-out culture should adopt Art Nouveau as its graphic style. Reproductions of Beardsley posters were on sale in several shops in 1964, and this must have suggested the poster as a cheap, mass-production way of disseminating or simply celebrating and indulging in the psychedelic culture.

Poster painters. Michael English (seated) and Nigel Waymouth with some of their prolific output. They have also made a record with their producer Guy Stevens (background). Behind English's head is the design for the record sleeve.

overleaf
'The Poster Scene', 1967.

Before the poster was commandeered as its main vehicle, the 'mind-expanding' art of this new underground was to be found on record jackets (a trend which would later reach its furthest fantasy in the design by Peter Blake and Jann Howarth for the sleeve of the Beatles' long-playing record 'Sergeant Pepper'), and in the pages of the *International Times* – the junkies' clarion, the American journal *Yarrow Roots*, which published pictures of copulating couples in its first issue, and the Australian magazine Oz, which more and more tended to abandon its original satiric function and to become a fantasy-sheet of artistic imagination. The principal posterists of the new style in 1966–7 were Michael English and Nigel Waymouth, both associated with the *International Times*, and the Australian artist Martin Sharp, who designed some open-out posters in the early issues of Oz, such as 'Toad of Whitehall' (Harold Wilson) and generally designed the magazine. In December 1967, *The Observer* published an acute article on 'Poster Power' by George Melly, together with a pen-portrait by Austin John Marshall of the American guitarist and pop-singer Jimi Hendrix, subject of some of the early pictorial rhapsodies of the psychedelic posterists. George Melly's article included an interview with English and Waymouth, who were working under the curious trade-name 'Hapshash and the Coloured Coat'. 'They are cool, polite, and very beautiful to look at with Harpo hair styles, un-ironed marbled shirts, tight trousers, loose belts and two-tone Cuban boots.' Mr Melly described how English, who had been at Ealing Art School, met Waymouth when the latter was painting the façade of the Kings Road, Chelsea, clothes boutique, 'Grannie Takes a Trip' in December 1966:

By March, 1967, they had decided to join forces and design posters. But what were these posters for? Superficially the answer was: to advertise the activities of U F O, which stands, among other things, for 'Unlimited Freak Out', and which was the first spontaneous and successful attempt to produce a total environment involving music, light and people.

What interested 'Hapshash' was *using* this environment as a launching pad. Unlike conventional poster-designers they weren't concerned with imposing their image on a product, but with taking their product out of the environment. It must be emphasized here that the aim of U F O was mind-expansion and hallucination at the service of the destruction of the non-hip and the substitution of 'love', in the special, rather nebulous meaning that the word holds for the Underground.

In the attempt to discover a visual equivalent, English and Waymouth had revived the use of 'Dayglo', a kind of luminous paint which gives weird effects in artificial light. Their lettering is described by Mr Melly as 'a rubbery synthesis of early Disney

275

Jimi Hendrix at home: the central icon figure of the modern decorative poster.

and Mabel Lucy Attwell carried to the edge of illegibility', while their pictorial style was 'almost a collage of other men's hard-won visions: Mucha, Ernst, Magritte, Bosch, William Blake, comic books, engravings of Red Indians, Disney, Dulac, ancient illustrations of treatises on alchemy: everything is boiled down to make a visionary and hallucinatory bouillabaisse.' The illegibility was significant: for the first time posters were being produced not for their message or advertisement value, but as works of art to hang on the domestic wall. Mr Melly does not say this in so many words, but he concludes: 'The Underground poster has succeeded in destroying the myth that the visual imagination has to be kept locked up in museums or imprisoned in heavy frames. It has helped open the eyes of a whole generation in the most literal sense.'

This could already be written less than a year after the first psychedelic posters were produced in England. But there was also a flourishing American school of underground posterists. An article was devoted to them in the January, 1967 issue of the San Francisco magazine *Ramparts.* A young man named Wes Wilson was claimed as the 'originator of the basic style', and with some coloured reproductions of convoluted and at times almost indecipherable posters there was also a photograph of two lugubrious bearded men who called themselves 'Mouse Studios' and were responsible for a cherry-and-purple design for the Avalon ballroom, while Wilson designed a mauve-and-royal-blue one for the Fillmore Auditorium. The magazine comments, whether with satiric intent I am not certain, 'That the lettering meanders all over the place with such abandon so that it takes considerable time and visual acrobatics to find out just what the words say is only a disadvantage in large advertising agencies and senior design classes in college.'

Posters such as 'Leap Year', by Osiris Visions Ltd., London, are sold in gramophone record shops and in 'poster boutiques' which sell little else. They can also be ordered through magazines like *Private Eye* – many of them sheer decoration, colour photographs of 'beach lovers' or 'nude dancers'; photographs and cartoons of the pandas who declined to mate at London Zoo; a reproduction of a 1943 Coca Cola advertisement glorifying American-Chinese friendship; and numberless personality-cult posters of Che Guevara, Vivaldi, Edward Lear and Chichester Fortescue, T. S. Eliot, Byron, or Auden and Isherwood standing in front of a smoker carriage on their way to America at the beginning of the Second World War. There have also been profitable offshoots of the poster industry, such as large cardboard postcards of famous writers, and cardboard coat hangers in the form of Jimi Hendrix, the Beatles and others.

Diane Marshall, a nineteen-year-
art student, won a competition to
design a poster for Tussaud's with
design in the manner of Roy
Lichtenstein, based on W. F. Yea
painting 'And when did you last
your father?'.

Peter Blake's design, also of 1968
commemorates the giant figure se
in Tussaud's entrance hall.

opposite Poster of Che Guevara,
published by the 'Revolution Pre

POUVOIR POPULAIRE

right and opposite Two student posters from the 'French Revolution' of May, 1968.

While these frivolous novelties were being turned out in England and America, the students of France, in the May Revolution of 1968, developed a new barebones poster style for anti-Gaullist and anti-police propaganda. With silkscreen and lithograph the student posterists, mostly anonymous, produced a series of utterly spontaneous designs which are as far removed from *le beau scholastique* as the poster is ever likely to get. Captions were scrawled freehand or excavated from the very body of the design – a perfect means of ensuring a message

283

opposite top The cartoonist Sempé became a hero of the Paris students by designing posters in their cause in 1968.

opposite bottom The battle of the posters: in Paris just before the 1969 referendum that caused de Gaulle's resignation, a huge 'Oui' poster has prophetically been covered with smaller 'Non' bills.

right 'His Master's Voice': one of the most effective Parisian student posters of 1968, satirizing de Gaulle's domination of the mass media.

integrated into the composition. In June, 1968, a portfolio of reproductions of these posters was published, edited by Jean Cassou. Several of them aim to unite the students and the workers. Others show the police as sinister, faceless truncheon-wielders. One of the most effective presents a goonish caricatured de Gaulle clutching a television set labelled 'La Voix de son Maître'. Another proclaims: 'Nous sommes tous indésirables', beneath the jubilant face of Daniel Cohn-Bendit. By these posters, says Cassou, the walls of Paris were 'magnificently profaned'.

opposite Wes Wilson: 'The Sound', a
San Francisco poster of 1966 for a pop
concert in the 'psychedelic' style.

Christopher Logue, himself responsible for a well-known English political poster, describes, in one of his 'true stories' in *Private Eye* of 13 September 1968, a significant incident of the May Revolution, which, he said, refutes the lie that 'art has no practical role to play in politics':

The absence of newspapers, radio, and television, allowed the poster to monopolize immediate communication. In next to no time thousands of posters began to appear all over the country giving aid and encouragement to the Revolution. In Paris, the best designed and the most efficiently produced posters came from the Ecole des Beaux Arts, the most famous art school in the West, whose ex-pupils include Poussin, David, Ingres, Seurat and so on. The CRS were told to go in and smash up the silk-screens on which the posters were being produced. Half an hour after the order had been signed they broke into the central courtyard of the school where they were faced by the students who were producing the posters. For once both sides were armed; the CRS with their usual stuff – gas, guns, clubs, shields, idiocy and hatred, and the students with no more than shields. But the CRS were stopped by their authorities, for the students shielded themselves and their silk screen with the fine collection of paintings bequeathed to the school by the late pupils Poussin, Ingres, David, Seurat et al. Here was a pretty pickle: 'millions of pounds' worth' of paintings against clubs. But as those clubs are the ultimate expression of 'millions of pounds' how could they destroy the very thing they were fighting to preserve. They withdrew.

The outrageous idea of Huysmans that Parisian posters could be preferred to Beaux-Arts paintings had now been translated into practical politics. When the Russians invaded Czechoslovakia in August, 1968, the students of Prague used the same summary poster techniques, graphic shorthand, in their 'cold resistance'.

History is beginning to be treated in decades rather than centuries. The chronicler of the 1960s will find in their posters an index to the fashions and ideas of youth. In the psychedelic posters, he will see the plumage and antics of the beautiful people; in the student posters of France and Czechoslovakia, the spirit of those who had to resist. In either case, he should get an attractive impression.

Bill Graham Presents
in San Francisco
THE SOUND
JEFFERSON AIRPLANE
MUDDY WATERS
FRI. SAT. FRI. SAT.
23·24·30·1
SEPT. SEPT. SEPT. OCT.
WINTERLAND
POST & STEINER
ADVANCE TICKETS $3.00
AT THE DOOR $3.50
9PM UNTIL 2PM
WES WILSON '66
BUTTERFIELD BLUES BAND
ALSO: TWO SUNDAY AFTERNOONS
SEPT. OCT.
25·2
FILLMORE AUDITORIUM $2.50
FILLMORE & GEARY STS.
FROM 2PM UNTIL 7PM
TICKETS
SAN FRANCISCO: City Lights Bookstore; The Psychedelic Shop; Bally Lo (Union Square); The Town Squire (1318 Polk); Mnasidika (1510 Haight) BERKELEY: Campus Records; Discount Records; Shakespeare & Co. MILL VALLEY: The Mod Hatter SAUSALITO: The Tides Bookstore; Rezall Pharmacy MENLO PARK: Kepler's Bookstore.

Select Bibliography

Abdy, Lady (Jane), *The French Poster: Chéret to Cappiello*, London, 1969.
American Federation of Arts, *The American Poster*, New York, 1967.
Amstutz, Walter, *Who's Who in Graphic Art*, Zurich, 1962.

Bella, Edward, *A Collection of Posters at the Royal Aquarium, London* (2 vols.) London, 1894–5, 1896.
Bergstrasser, G., *Katalog der Plakat-Sammlung des ... Landesmuseums ... zu der Ausstellung*, Darmstadt, 1962.
Biegeleisen, Jacob Israel, *Poster Design*, New York, 1945.
Bilbo, Jack *(pseud.)*, *Toulouse-Lautrec and Steinlen*, London, 1946.
Boudet, M. G., *Les affiches étrangères, 1896–7*, Paris, 1898.
Bradshaw, Percy V., *Art in Advertising*, London, 1924. *The Art of the Illustrator*, London, 1918.
Breitenbach, Edgar, *The Poster Craze; the American Heritage*, New York, 1962.
Browse, Lillian, *William Nicholson*, London, 1956.

Cecil, Lord David, *Max* (Beerbohm), London, 1964.
Cleugh, James, *Charles B. Cochran, Lord Bountiful*, New York, 1938.
Cochran, Sir Charles B., *Cock-a-doodle-do*, London, 1941.
    I had almost forgotten, London, 1932. *Secrets of a Showman*, London, 1925. *Showman Looks On*, London, 1945.
Commander, John, *Seventeen Graphic Designers*, London, 1963.
Connolly, L., *Posters and American War Posters, historical and explanatory*, Newark, USA, 1917.
Conway, Sir M., *L.M.S. Railway Posters*, London, 1926.
Cooper, Austin, *Making a Poster*, London, 1938.
Cooper, Douglas, *Henri de Toulouse-Lautrec, 1864–1901*, London, 1952.
Crauzat, E. de, *L'Œuvre Gravi et Lithographié de Steinlen*, Paris, 1913.

Des Ombiaux, M., *Quatre artistes liégeois*, Paris, 1907.
Dooijes, Dick, *A history of the Dutch poster, 1890–1960*, Amsterdam, 1968.
(The author regrets that this excellent work only came to his notice when the present book was at an advanced stage.)

Eckersley, Tom, *Poster Design*, London, 1954.

Fougasse (Cyril Kenneth Bird), '*... and the Gatepost*', London, 1940.
    A School of Purposes, A Selection of Fougasse Posters, 1939–45, London, 1946.
Frenzel, H. K., *Ludwig Hohlwein und Sein Werk*, Berlin, 1938.

Games, Abram, *Over My Shoulder*, London, 1960.
Gandhilon, R., *Classement, catalogage et conservation des affiches*, Châlons-sur-Marne, 1953.
Gasser, Manuel, *Herbert Leupin: Plakate*, Zurich, 1957.
Grand-Carteret, John, *Vieux Papiers, Vieilles Images; Cartons d'un Collectionneur*, Paris, 1896.
Griessmaier, V., *Österreichische Plakate, 1890–1957*, Vienna, 1957.
Graves, Charles P. R., *The Cochran Story*, 1951.

Hardie, Martin, *War Posters, 1914–19*, London, 1920.
Hasluck, Paul N., *How to write signs, tickets, and posters*, London, 1901.
Havinden, Ashley, *Advertising and the Artist*, London, 1956.
Herzfelde, Wieland, *John Heartfield, Leben und Werke*, Dresden, 1962.
Hiatt, Charles, *Picture Posters*, London, 1895.
Hudson, Derek, *James Pryde, 1866–1941*, London, 1949.
Hutchinson, Harold F., *London Transport Posters*, London, 1963.
    The poster: an illustrated history from 1860, London, 1968.

Johnson, A. E., *Dudley Hardy*, London, 1907. *John Hassall*, London, 1907.

Jones, Sydney R., *Posters and their designers*, London, 1924.
Julien, Edouard, *Les affiches de Toulouse-Lautrec*, Paris, 1950.

Kasser, Hans, *Das Schweizer Plakat*, Zurich, 1950.
Kauffer, E. McKnight, *The Art of the Poster*, London, 1924.

Laver, James, *Art for All: London Transport Posters, 1908–49*, London, 1949.
   Nineteenth-century French posters, London, 1944.
Lo Duca, Joseph M., *L'affiche*, Paris, 1947.

Maclean, Ruari, *The Wood Engravings of Joan Hassall*, London, 1960.
Maindron, Ernest, *Les Affiches Illustrées*, Paris, 1887 and 1896.
Mauclair, Camille, *Jules Chéret*, Paris, 1930.
Metzl, Ervine, *The Poster, its History and its Art*, New York, 1963.
Mourlot, Fernand, *The original Posters of Braque, Chagall, etc.*, Monte Carlo and London, 1959.
Mucha, Jiří, *Alphonse Mucha*, London, 1967.

Plietzsch, *Lucian Bernhard*, The Hague, 1913.
Pollard, Percival, *Posters in Miniature*, New York, 1896.
Price, C. Matlock, *Poster Designers*, New York, 1922.
Purnell's *History of the Second World War*, 1968.
Purnell's *History of the Twentieth Century*, 1968, in particular,
   an article by Lord Francis-Williams, 'Propaganda 1914–15'.
Purvis, Tom, *Poster Progress*, London, 1939.

Rademacher, Hellmut, *Das Deutsche Plakat*, Dresden, 1965.
Rati Opizzoni, Count C. A., *Armand Rassenfosse nella vita e nell'opera*, Milan, 1915.
Reade, Brian, *Art Nouveau and Alphonse Mucha*, London 1963, *Beardsley*, London and New York, 1967.
Rickards, Maurice, *Posters of the 1920s*, London, 1968. *Posters of the First World War*, London, 1968.
Rogers, W. S., *A Book of the Poster*, London, 1901.
Rotzler, W., *Meister der Plakatkunst*, Zurich, 1959.

Sailer, Anton, *Das Plakat*, Munich, 1956.
Sampson, H., *A History of Advertising*, London, 1874.
Sheldon, Cyril, *A History of Poster Advertising*, London, 1937.
Sparrow, W. S., *Advertising and British Art*, London, 1924.
Sponsel, J. L., *Das Moderne Plakat*, Dresden, 1897.
Steen, Marguerite, *William Nicholson*, 1943.

Turner, E. S., *The Shocking History of Advertising*, London, 1952.
Typophiles of New York, *Will Bradley: His Chap-Book* (Bradley's autobiography), New York, 1955.

Vox, Maximilien, *A. M. Cassandre, Plakate*, St Gallen, 1948.

Wagner, C., *Senefelder*, Leipzig, 1914.
Wascher, H., *Das Deutsche Illustrierte Flugblatt*, Dresden, 1955–6.
Wember, Paul, *Die Jugend der Plakate*, 1887–1917, Krefeld, 1961.
Wintsch, G., *Un artiste lausannois*, Paris, 1919.

Zur Westen, Walter von, *Krieg, Kriegerstand und Gebrauchsgraphik: Berlin
   Verein der Plakatfreunde*, 1915. *Reklamekunst*, Leipzig, 1903.

JOURNALS   *Les Maîtres de l'Affiche* (5 vols) Paris, 1896–1900.
The Poster (4 vols) London, 1898–1900. *Das Plakat*, Charlottenburg, Berlin, 1920.

Acknowledgements

*The author and publishers would like to thank the trustees
and owners of the museums and collections listed below for
granting permission for the photographs to be reproduced.*

50 (*bottom*), Agence Braun, Paris; 40, Amsterdam Printen Kabinet;
57, 74, Bibliothèque des Arts Décoratifs, Paris; 99, collection of Peter
and Jann Blake; 204/5, Joachim Blauel, Munich; 10, 21, 29, 30, 31,
42, 43, 47, 72, 73, 103, 106, 115, 122, 130, 133, 134, 139, 140, 141,
144, 146, 147, 153, 155, 156, 158, 161, 164, 165, 167, 168, 169, 170,
173, 201, 210, 211, British Museum; 75, collection of Victoria Brittain;
278 (Terence Donovan/*Observer*), 274, 276/7 (Patrick Ward/*Observer*),
Camera Press Ltd; 273, Copyrun Ltd; 48, collection of Richard
Dennis; 193 (*right*), 195, 199, Deutsche Fotothek, Dresden; 116, Fine
Art Society, London; 50 (*top*), Galerie Charpentier, Paris; 184/5,
Haaga Gemeentesmuseum, Holland; 83 (*top and bottom*), 84 (*top
and bottom*), 93 (*top*), collection of Joan Hassall; 78, 114, collection
of Victor Hutchings; 225, 226, 227, 229, 232, 234, 240, 241, 242, 244,
Imperial War Museum, London; 182, 192 (*top and bottom*), 222, 251,
Kaiser Wilhelm Museum, Krefeld; 285 (*bottom*), Keystone Press;
272, Kleptomania, London; 193 (*left*), 196, 197 (*top and bottom*),
221, 238, Landesmuseum Baden-Württemberg, Stuttgart; 28,32,34,37,
38, 41, 44, 46, 52, 53, 54/5, 60/61, 63, 64, 65, 68, 69, 76, 77, 80, 87,
89, 90, 94/5, 102, 108, 128, 137, 148, 154, 162, 166, 172, 178/9, 181,
188, 194, 198, 203, 206 (*left and right*), 207, 213, 230, 235, 239, 248
(*top and bottom*), 252, 253, 255 (*top, left and right, bottom*), 256, 257,
258, 259, 263, 265, 266, 282, 287, Lords Gallery, London; 280 (*top
and bottom*), Madame Tussaud's, London; 159, 160, 171, New York
Public Library; 269, Osiris Visions Ltd, London; 271, Philips Ltd,
London; 14, 20, 22, 26, 27, 58, 62, 67, 70/71, 79, 93 (*bottom*), 104,
110, 112, 118, 119, 120, 121, 124, 125, 126, 127, 132, 142, 150, 151,
157, 176, 177, 187, 189, 208, 209 (*left and right*), 212, 215, 216, 217,
The Poster; 245, collection of Dora Raeburn; 281, Revolution Press;
218, 220, 223, G. Ricordi and Sons, Milan; 13, John Rylands Library,
Manchester; 18, by permission of Studio Vista, London; 283, 284, 285
(*top*), Tchou, Paris; 128, 163, 175, 190, 200, Victoria and Albert
Museum, London.

Index

ÉCOLE D'APPR

COCHERS